# Growing in CHRiST®

## High School
## Teacher Guide

CONCORDIA PUBLISHING HOUSE · SAINT LOUIS

# God Creates a World and a People

Copyright © 2014, 2016 Concordia Publishing House
3558 S. Jefferson Ave., St. Louis, MO 63118-3968
1-800-325-3040 • www.cph.org

Written by Michelle Bauman, Elizabeth Foreman, and Cynthia A. Wheeler

Edited by Cynthia A. Wheeler

Manufactured in the United States of America

Growing in Christ® is published by Concordia Publishing House. Your comments and suggestions concerning this material are appreciated. Email us at sundayschool@cph.org.

# Contents

# Introduction

The High School level for youth in ninth through twelfth grades includes this Teacher Guide and reproducible Student Pages.

## Teacher Guide Features

- **Preparing the Lesson pages** give you background and theological information.
- **Four-step lessons** make preparation and teaching easy and effective.
- **Activity-based openings** engage youth in lessons.
- **Small-group/large-group activity options** dig into God's Word and share faith. Do activities in ways that make the most sense for your group.
- **YouTube videos** encourage critical thinking and discernment.
- **"We Live" activities** help young people identify personal applications in worship and living as God's children.
- **Reproducible Student Pages** focus Bible learning and discussions.
- **Perforated pages** make team teaching or small-group/large-group teaching easier.
- **Timeline Poster** promotes biblical and historical perspectives and insights.

## Your Role as Teacher

As a teacher, you challenge, coach, encourage creativity and curiosity, and nurture students' faith in Jesus. Building positive relationships with and between teens is very important. Welcome students as they arrive. Find out names of those you do not know. Encourage students to become comfortable. Get to know your students and their families.

Young people may feel wary of trying new things, fearing embarrassment. Provide a safe space for everyone to participate by not allowing put-downs, hurtful jokes, name calling, or other improper suggestions.

Model the behavior you want from students by participating yourself and enthusiastically introducing activities. Each time students participate, trust builds. Trust makes students more willing to read aloud, do activities and tasks, participate in small groups, pray together, and share opinions, feelings, and group work.

Make your classroom a place where students can talk openly and share struggles. Remind students to respect one another's privacy. Say you will not share their stories outside of class. However, if a student shares something potentially dangerous to self or others, you have the responsibility to bring it to your pastor for guidance.

Students look up and read the primary Scripture each week. Extra verses printed on Student Pages make it easier for students to use and discuss them. Rarely, lessons ask students to look up extra verses. To help newcomers, provide copies of the Bible in the same version and jot down page numbers, or bookmark pages with paper strips ahead of time to make it easier to find Bible references. Explain chapter and verse numbers, as needed.

## Other Supplies

Before class, collect items in the "Get Ready" section of your lesson. This list always includes Bibles and reproducible Student Pages. Most lessons use pens or pencils, masking tape, newsprint, and markers. A few lessons suggest other supplies.

Find additional teaching help, including curriculum and video updates, training, links to podcasts, and other resources, at our Sunday School website, **www.cph.org/sundayschool**.

# YouTube Resources for These Lessons

Go to the CPH Youth Sunday School Resources page at **bit.ly/1knXwnU**. Choose "Old Testament 1 High School Playlist," and then click the name of the video to play it. View or skip ads and cue the video. Channels may block or hinder play if you do not watch the ads.

YouTube settings change often. **If a video is not available, go to cph.org/sundayschool and click "Sunday School Tools" on the main page. Click "Curriculum Updates" for another option.**

### Lesson 1: God Creates the World
"What Is the Evidence for the Big Bang?" Fraser Cain channel (5:27; stop 4:14)

### Lesson 2: God Creates Adam and Eve
"Making the Solar System," To Scale channel (3:25)

### Lesson 3: Sin Enters the World
"Filled," Igniter Media channel (2:55)

### Lesson 4: Cain and Abel
"Jedi Kittens Strike Back," Final Cut King channel (0:51)

### Lesson 5: Noah and the Flood
"Rescued," Igniter Media channel (2:34)

### Lesson 6: God's Covenant with Abram
"New Covenant (Yeshua) Joshua Aaron | Messianic Music" Joshua Aaron channel (3:01)

### Lesson 7: Abraham's Visitors from Heaven
"Paul Walker—Do People Become Angels?" Living Waters / The Way of the Master channel (2:07)

### Lesson 8: Abraham and Isaac
"Christiano Ronaldo and Son - A father's story" Nameless channel (3:52; start :09, stop 3:28)

### Lesson 9: Isaac and Rebekah
"That's Amore," Central Films channel (3:15)

### Lesson 10: Jacob and Esau
"Surprising Facts About: Twins," Thoughty2 channel (7:26; play 5:58–6:58)

### Lesson 11: Jacob's Dream
"The True Story of Kid President," Soul Pancake channel (4:22; stop 4:05)

### Lesson 12: Jacob's Family
"The Radford Family | Where you belong" from AccordingTooYouxx channel (2:00)

### Lesson 13: Esau Forgives Jacob
"Kid President's 25 Reasons To Be Thankful!" Soul Pancake channel (3:47; stop 3:10)

# Lesson 1

# Preparing the Lesson

## God Creates the World

Genesis 1:1–2:3

Date of Use

## Key Point

God made the world in six days by the power of His Word. All creation is God's blessing to us.

## Law/Gospel

God requires that I believe that He is the only true God, the Creator and Sustainer of the world. **God gives me faith to believe that He created the earth and heavens, and He continues to provide me with all that I need to sustain this body and life, including forgiveness for my sins, through His Son, Jesus Christ.**

## Context

Genesis is a family history about Abraham, Isaac, and Jacob (called Israel), chosen by God. The creation account and other material in Genesis 1–11 serves as foundation for the family history that follows in Genesis 12–50.

Moses is the authority behind the first five books of the Bible, called the Torah (Law). Some material was revealed directly to Moses; other material was known to generations before Moses and, under the guidance of the Holy Spirit, was set down by him or immediate successors.

The Genesis accounts of creation, the preflood world, the flood, and the immediate resettlement after the flood have parallels in ancient writings that predate Moses, particularly in Mesopotamia.

## Commentary

The Spirit of God hovering over the waters of the formless void shows that the Spirit brings order out of chaos. This image recurs in the Baptism of Christ (Mark 1:10), where it reminds us that in Christ we are a new creation (2 Corinthians 5:17), with the Spirit bringing order out of our chaos. The Hebrew word translated "Spirit" in Genesis 1:2 also means "wind" or "breath."

Words are formed from breath. As God proceeds to speak creation into being, the Genesis account establishes a unity between God the speaker, the Word by which He created the world, and the Spirit. This Word became flesh in Christ Jesus, as proclaimed in John 1:1–14. The words of Psalm 104:30 also portray the Spirit as an agent of creation. God's Word does what it says ("Let there be . . . and there was"). What God declares is true; God's Word is truth (John 17:17).

God begins His creation by creating light on the first day. God is the real source of light. Each day, God adds dramatically to the world that He calls "good"—heaven; earth and seas; plants; sun, moon, and stars; creatures that swim and fly; creatures that walk and crawl on the ground; and finally, man, both male and female. Some mistakenly worship the sun or other elements of creation that merely do what God assigns to them. However, they were not made to be worshiped but to be used.

The creation of people on the sixth day serves as the climax of creation. God creates both male and female in His image. Our image is not physical likeness but spiritual likeness, or righteousness. Note that man's rule over all other creatures and marriage/procreation are part of the sinless creation, which God declares "very good." God gives plants as food; death for humans and animals is not part of this perfect creation. Everything is intended to work for good.

Because God rested on the seventh day (our Saturday), the Sabbath ("rest") day was set apart ("made holy"). The ceremonial laws regarding the Sabbath have their fulfillment in Christ, who, having finished His work on Good Friday (John 19:30), rested in the tomb on the Sabbath. Christians from the earliest times met on Sundays to celebrate His resurrection. The commandment concerning the Sabbath no longer pertains to a particular day of the week but rather to setting aside time so that God might re-create us through His Word. Creation's patterns give us a sense of how things "ought to be."

**To hear an in-depth discussion of this Bible account, visit cph.org/podcast and listen to our Seeds of Faith podcast each week.**

Lesson 1

# God Creates the World

Genesis 1:1–2:3

## Get Ready
### Before Class

- Copy Student Page 1 for each person.

- For **Opening**, preview the Lesson 1 YouTube video in the Old Testament 1 High School playlist at **bit.ly/1knXwnU**. To use it, get equipment ready (e.g., computer, tablet, Internet connection) and cue the video.

  Hang up 3 newsprint sheets with masking tape and get markers. Add a word at the top of each in order from left to right: *Evidence; Assumptions; Conclusions.* On the Evidence sheet, write *open cookie jar, no cookies, crumbs on counter.*

  Get pencils or pens.

- For **God Speaks**, get Bibles and the Timeline Poster. Hang up 3–4 newsprint sheets.

## 1 Opening (20 minutes)

### Expanding Our Universe

Use this activity to help students identify evidence and assumptions that inform conclusions and theories. Often, people look for evidence to support their beliefs; and then they interpret the evidence with assumptions that lead to flawed conclusions and theories.

Gather near the newsprint sheets. In three to five minutes, read and discuss the cookie situation on the *Evidence* newsprint sheet (prepared as directed in Get Ready).

**Ask** **Based on this evidence, what assumptions could we make?** Jot student responses on the *Assumption* sheet. Prompt students to think of different assumptions the evidence entertains, such as an intruder ate the cookies, the cookies disintegrated, or there were no cookies in the first place.

**Our assumptions may or may not be true, but what conclusions could we make based on our evidence and assumptions?** Write a theory for each assumption on the *Conclusions* sheet.

**Which conclusion is most likely? Why?** Circle it and discuss.

**What could people who don't agree with the majority opinion do?** The minority could protest, issue a separate opinion, be ignored, or withdraw.

If you choose not to use the video, use the notes below to lead a discussion of one kind of evidence or jump to the "Ask" section.

If you use the video, hand out copies of Student Page 1 and pencils or pens.

**Say** **Today, we study what God's Word says about creation and compare it to scientific theories. In this video, Fraser Cain, editor of the *Universe Today* website, cites four kinds of evidence for the big bang theory. Jot evidence, assumptions, conclusions, and theories on the back of your paper.**

Show the Lesson 1 YouTube video, "What Is the Evidence for the Big Bang?" (5:27, stop at 4:14), in the Old Testament 1 High School playlist at **bit.ly/1knXwnU**. You can find a transcript of the video in the comment section below it.

Then let students choose one of the four kinds of evidence the video stated for the big bang (listed below). Write *big bang* on the *Theory* newsprint sheet. Discuss the video claims and identify assumptions and conclusions, writing them on correlating newsprint sheets. Some things cited as evidence are actually assumptions or conclusions.

Use the following notes about the video content to assist your discussion.

**Growing in CHRIST.**

## Four Kinds of Evidence Cited to Support the Big Bang Theory

**1** **The universe is expanding** (conclusion, not evidence)**.** Evidence includes measuring changes in wavelengths of light to calculate the *assumed* speed and direction of spiral galaxies, and differences in energy output and time between pulses of pulsing stars. Both *assume* the speed of light has stayed the same after the *assumed* big bang. We have measured the speed of light for fewer than four hundred years. What if light traveled faster or slower in an earlier time?

**2** **An abundance of elements** (evidence)**.** Cain said that right after the big bang, "hydrogen compressed into a tiny volume with crazy heat and pressure" (theory). Measurements of hydrogen and other trace elements (evidence) exactly match *expected* results if the universe was once a big star (assumption). Could other factors, perhaps yet unknown, affect these elements?

**3** **Cosmic microwave background radiation** comes from every direction (evidence). The theory *assumes* a massive radiation release from the big bang billions of years ago that shifted from visible light to background radiation (conclusion/theory) as it traveled away. Could something else cause it? And why does it come from all directions, instead of moving in one direction?

**4** **The formation of galaxies and large-scale structures** of the cosmos (evidence) shows a cooling universe (conclusion/theory) where gravity (evidence) pulled these structures together (conclusion/theory).

## Disputed Scientific Theories

Cain misleadingly said, "Almost all astronomers agree on the theories of the big bang." However, many physicists do not agree with the big bang theory. They also do not agree on a "unified field" theory to explain gravity, special relativity, electromagnetism, and other mysteries. Einstein's original theory of general relativity has been revised and continues to be modified by current research.

In addition, evolution has largely been discredited by the study of DNA, the complexity of cells and systems, the fossil record, and probability theory. (Source: "What Your Atheist Professor Doesn't Know [But Should]" by Stephen Joseph Williams [CreateSpace Publishing, 2009–14].)

See a list of over eight hundred scientists skeptical about Darwinian evolution online at dissentfromdarwin.org, including Nobel Prize winners.

**Ask** **Name some scientific theories that were discredited in the past.** The flat earth; earth-centric solar system instead of sun-centered; location of the planet Vulcan between Mercury and the sun; spontaneous generation; Mars canals; blank-slate personality theory; and that stress, not bacteria, causes ulcers are just a few.

**What assumptions or conclusions do Christians make about the Genesis account of God's creation?** Christians believe the Bible is God's true Word without error. We consider Genesis 1 a historical account, not a science textbook, myth, or poetry (as in creation imagery in Psalm 104:5–9).

We see evidence of God's creation in our complex, finely tuned world, our intricate bodies, and the vast universe (natural revelation). Based on God's Word, we believe (conclude/trust) that God created it (special revelation).

**Pray** **Heavenly Father, You richly give and sustain life and provide food and shelter for all living things. Forgive us when we fail to recognize Your work. Open our eyes to know You as Author and Creator of all and to recognize Your work in our lives. In Christ's name we pray. Amen.**

## Key Point

God made the world in six days by the power of His Word. All creation is God's blessing to us.

*Goes to the Heart*

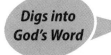

God made the world in six days by the power of His Word. All creation is God's blessing to us.

**Digs into God's Word**

# 2 God Speaks (22 minutes)

## Witnesses to God's Creative Work

Hand out Bibles. Ask a volunteer to act as a scribe who will write what God did in the seven days of creation on a sheet of newsprint.

Then ask students to take turns reading verses of **Genesis 1:1–2:3**. As you do, help your scribe list the things God created each day on the newsprint. When done, thank your scribe and ask him or her to sit down.

These initial questions are not on the Student Page.

**Ask** **What observations can you make about this Scripture?** Students might observe different things as they look at the newsprint lists and Scripture.

Based on their comments, discuss the following information.

- Before God created, there was nothing. The Latin word *ex nihilo* means "out of nothing." Interestingly, this is what the opening video said big-bang theorists think existed before the beginning.

- However, most physicists acknowledge they do not know what existed previously. Early in his career, Albert Einstein thought the universe was eternal with no beginning. He was Jewish, not an atheist, as many claim.

- Genesis shows God's organized and orderly work, not chaos.

- God first created light. Remind students of the video's premise that the universe started in one place as a large star (light). God created heaven next.

- God created vegetation before He set up the moon and the sun, which provides light for plants to grow. But, remember light was already created.

- The order in which God created creatures matches closely with scientific suggestions: water creatures, birds; livestock, creeping things, beasts; humans.

- The Hebrew verb for "create" is used in the Bible only to describe God's work, never human's, affirming that only God truly creates out of nothing.

- Principles of scriptural interpretation consider the literature type (in this case, historical), context of immediate verses, the book (Genesis), other writings by the same author (Moses), and all of Scripture; and use the most obvious word meaning, unless context and literature type suggest otherwise.
  Our church teaches that each day was a literal twenty-four-hour day. A study of other places in Scripture that use the Hebrew words translated as *day*, *morning*, and *evening* also usually use these common meanings.

- Some Christians believe creation took longer than seven days to make it more compatible with science. However, we should not change Scripture to fit our ideas. While facts prove many aspects of Scripture, we do not base our faith on human validation of these facts.

- Rather, the Holy Spirit leads us to believe God's creation account in Genesis 1 as true. Christians believe it by faith (Hebrews 11:3) because God said it in His true Holy Word, the Bible, which is without errors.

- For those interested in further study, suggest this helpful, small book: *In the Beginning, God: Creation from God's Perspective* by Joel Heck (CPH 2011).

**Ask** **How did God create?** God spoke to create. ("God said.")

**What did God say about His creation?** It was good, very good.

**What blessing did God give the animals first, and then people (vv. 22, 28)?** "Be fruitful and multiply." He added for people to subdue the earth and have dominion over other creatures.

If you haven't done so, hand out Student Page 1 copies and continue using it.

Ask volunteers to read **Genesis 1:2** again and **John 1** verses (on Student Page).

**Ask** We call God the Father "Creator," but He wasn't alone in the beginning. **Who else was at creation? What did They do?** The Holy Spirit hovered over the waters. God created all things through the Word, His Son.

**Who is the true light? How and why did He come into the world?** Jesus is the light of the world (John 8:12). He came as a humble, helpless baby to be our Savior, to die on the cross to pay for our sins, and to rise from the dead to give us new life with our triune God, now and forever.

**God created all things through Christ, the Word. What else do we receive through Jesus (John 1:12)?** Jesus gives all who receive Him and believe in His name the right to be called children of God. The Holy Spirit works through Baptism and God's Word to give us faith and make us God's children.

**How do we know that the creation account in Genesis is true? Read 2 Timothy 3:16–17 and 2 Peter 1:21 (on Student Page).** These verses reinforce the power and truth of God's Word. We believe the Bible is God's Spirit-inspired Word and accept the creation account as truth. Believing in the inspiration of Scripture means trusting the Word as written. If we question creation, we also call the resurrection of Christ into question, in whom our hope resides.

Question 3 in *Luther's Small Catechism with Explanation* says, "The Bible is the 'Holy Scripture' because God the Holy Spirit gave to His chosen writers the thoughts that they expressed and the words that they wrote (verbal inspiration). Therefore, the Bible is God's own Word and truth, without error (inerrancy)."

*Goes to the Heart*

# **3 We Live** (15 minutes)

## The World Says . . .

Discuss one or more of the four statements on the Student Page, helping students apply what they learned from Scripture today. These statements contain basics of the theory of evolution, which contradicts the Word of God.

**1 The world began with a chaotic big bang.** Evolution maintains life was created by accident; out of chaos, life began and progressed to what it is today. However, we believe our world was not created by pure chance or random accident. We observe great order in the universe. Our world and all its creatures are too complex to evolve by chance.

Nature maintains rhythms and patterns passed from season to season and from one generation to the next. Our cells use elaborate systems, intricate sequences, and complex combinations of proteins, bacteria, and other substances.

Roger Penrose, British mathematician and co-worker/friend of Stephen Hawking calculated the probability of an orderly universe coming out of the big bang as 1 in $10^{123}$ (one followed by 123 zeroes). However, probability theorists say anything less than 1 in $10^{50}$ is impossible. (Source: Williams, p. 126.)

**Faith in Action**
Tell students that in today's lesson, we see the triune God at work for us from the beginning. We say the Invocation at the beginning of worship in the name of the one true God—Father, Son, and Holy Spirit. Confessing faith in the triune God reminds us of our Baptism in His name.

**2** **Death is nature's way of ensuring the survival of the fittest.** Evolution sees death as natural and necessary for the survival of the fittest. Christians believe death is a consequence of sin (Romans 6:23; Genesis 3:19). God is not the author of evil but the giver of life. God's basic attributes make evolution impossible.

**3** **Plants and animals evolved over time and eventually developed into new species.** God made animals and plants unique in their own way. Scientists observe microevolution within species, small changes, and adaptations.

However, macroevolution, where one species turns into another, has never been observed. Darwin's theory depends on mutations happening often and with positive results. Instead, we observe mutations happening one at a time, not in bunches, and usually bringing negative, not positive results. For example, a genetic mutation causes progeria, which causes accelerated aging.

Probability theorists also say there isn't enough time for life to evolve with Darwin's mutations. According to prominent evolutionist Dr. Francisco Ayala from the University of California, Irvine, the chance of humans evolving from bacteria is 1 in 10 to the one millionth power. Remember, more than 1 in $10^{50}$ is impossible. (Source: Williams, pp. 176–77.)

In his book *The Cell's Design: How Chemistry Reveals the Creator's Artistry*, Dr. Fazale Rana cites over one hundred examples of startling similarities of biologically unrelated creatures that could not have evolved similar features through separate branches of life. Examples include the similar structure of bird and bat wings, who do not have a genetic connection to a common ancestor. (Source: Williams, pp. 175–77.)

**4** **Humans descended from apes.** Scripture says that God created humans in a special way and gave them souls (next week's lesson). We did not evolve from another mammal.

Ask volunteers to read **Romans 1:20–22** (Student Page).

**Ask** **How do these verses shine light on our lesson?** God's creation shows the reality of His existence. When we see our magnificent world, the size of the universe, and the complexity of the human body, we realize someone had to create it. Orderly, systematic processes do not spring up from nothing.

Things do not naturally get better, especially without intervention. Instead, things decay and degrade. People who fail to see God's work in creation and who don't seek to know Him through His Word become futile and foolish in their thinking.

As scientists learn more about the complexity of God's creation and the tiny variations in the many parameters that sustain life, more conclude that there must be an intelligent mind involved in its design.

**How does God richly and daily provide all you need to support your body and life?** God's Word is powerful. God promises to care for our physical and spiritual needs. Through God's Word and Sacraments, the Holy Spirit creates faith in the one true triune God. By grace through faith in Christ Jesus, who died for our sins and rose from the dead, we receive forgiveness of sin and eternal life. In faith, we trust God to provide all we need for daily life.

*Goes to
the Heart*

**Say** **We have not always seen God as our Creator or been good stewards of His gifts. Despite our sin, God adopted us as His children in Baptism and forgives our sins in Christ Jesus. May He keep us in the true faith by His grace and mercy.**

# 4 Closing (3 minutes)

**Ask** **What evidence, assumption, conclusion, or theory most surprised you today?** Thank students who share.

**Name something you want to know more about.** Thank students who share.

To close, read aloud together the First Article of the Apostles' Creed and its meaning from Luther's Small Catechism (Student Page).

## Lesson 1
# God creates the world

Genesis 1:1–2:3

## Witnesses to God's creative work

Read **Genesis 1:2** again and these **John 1** verses.

**John 1:1–4, 9–12, 14:** In the beginning was the Word, and the Word was with God, and the Word was God. 2 He was in the beginning with God. 3 All things were made through Him, and without Him was not any thing made that was made. 4 In Him was life, and the life was the light of men. . . .

9 The true light, which gives light to everyone, was coming into the world. 10 He was in the world, and the world was made through Him, yet the world did not know Him. 11 He came to His own, and His own people did not receive him. 12 But to all who did receive Him, who believed in His name, He gave the right to become children of God. . . .

14 And the Word became flesh and dwelt among us, and we have seen His glory, glory as of the only Son from the Father, full of grace and truth.

- We call God the Father "Creator," but He wasn't alone in the beginning. Who else was at creation? What did They do?

- Who is the true light? How and why did He come into the world?

- God created all things through Christ, the Word. What else do we receive through Jesus (John 1:12)?

- How do we know that the creation account in Genesis is true?

**2 Timothy 3:16–17:** All Scripture is breathed out by God and profitable for teaching, for reproof, for correction, and for training in righteousness, that the man of God may be complete, equipped for every good work.

**2 Peter 1:21:** For no prophecy was ever produced by the will of man, but men spoke from God as they were carried along by the Holy Spirit.

## The world says . . .

Using God's Word, refute these false teachings.

1. The world began with a chaotic big bang.

2. Death is nature's way of ensuring the survival of the fittest.

3. Plants and animals evolved over time and eventually developed into new species.

4. Humans descended from apes.

- How do these verses shine light on our lesson?

**Romans 1:20–22:** For [God's] invisible attributes, namely, His eternal power and divine nature, have been clearly perceived, ever since the creation of the world, in the things that have been made. So they are without excuse. For although they knew God, they did not honor Him as God or give thanks to Him, but they became futile in their thinking, and their foolish hearts were darkened. Claiming to be wise, they became fools.

## God creates today

How does God richly and daily provide all you need to support your body and life?

### The First Article of the Apostles' Creed: Creation

I believe in God, the Father Almighty, Maker of heaven and earth.

*What does this mean?*

I believe that God has made me and all creatures; that He has given me my body and soul, eyes, ears, and all my members, my reason and all my senses, and still takes care of them.

He also gives me clothing and shoes, food and drink, house and home, wife and children, land, animals, and all I have. He richly and daily provides me with all that I need to support this body and life.

He defends me against all danger and guards and protects me from all evil.

All this He does only out of fatherly, divine goodness and mercy, without any merit or worthiness in me. For all this it is my duty to thank and praise, serve and obey Him.

This is most certainly true.

# Preparing the Lesson

## God Creates Adam and Eve

Genesis 1:26–2:25

## Key Point

God has made us in His image, provides all things for our good, and makes us rulers over the earth and everything in it.

## Law/Gospel

God appoints me as a caretaker of His creation and expects me to take care of it for His glory and the good of others. **God provides me with all good things for this life and forgives me for Jesus' sake when I put myself above Him and His creation or when I misuse or neglect my vocation to rule the earth properly.**

## Context

Some have argued that Genesis 2 is a second account of creation. But Genesis 2 presupposes the five preceding days of creation. This chapter reviews in more detail the creation of mankind in Adam and Eve.

## Commentary

The name Adam means "earth" and points to humanity's material aspect. But the "breath," or "spirit," of God makes Adam a living being and gives him fellowship with God. God is the source of life—turning away from that source leads to death. Having God's Spirit in Genesis 2 corresponds to being made in the image of God in Genesis 1. The earthly blessings that follow express the love God has for Adam.

Eden is sometimes called "Paradise" (garden). The tree of life within Eden may have been planted near running or "living" water—as in Psalm 1:3. Note that the tree of life and living water are linked again in Revelation 22:1–2.

The tree of the knowledge of good and evil is sometimes identified as an apple tree because the Latin words for *evil* and *apple* share the same root, *mal.* Jewish tradition pictures the tree of the knowledge of good and evil as a citron tree or a grapevine. But the actual fruit is never identified in Scripture.

Four rivers flow from around Eden, including two that were the mainstay of Mesopotamian life and civilization: the Tigris and the Euphrates. The locations of the other two rivers have not been identified, perhaps due to changes to the earth's surface during the worldwide flood later in Genesis.

Man is given the task of working the garden. To this day, work, or vocation, remains one of our innate needs. Adam's naming of the animals shows mastery as well as intelligence.

Note the underlying pattern, hierarchy, and priority. There are things above and below; all things are good, but some are better—or could be better. Adam in Paradise needs a "suitable helper." The woman is created from his flesh so that he will care for her as for himself. Moses issues a command: "Therefore a man shall leave his father and his mother and hold fast to his wife, and they shall become one flesh" (Genesis 2:24). The marriage relationship has priority even over parental obligations.

The man and woman were naked and without shame. They were open and trusting, with nothing to hide. A child with beautiful freckles may be made ashamed due to hurtful comments and insults and then may internalize that shame. Shame arises from evil without as well as from evil within; Paradise was free of both. Living according to God's Law brings earthly blessing. The man Adam foreshadows Christ, the new Adam (Romans 5:12–21), who brings believers into eternal paradise (Luke 23:43).

**To hear an in-depth discussion of this Bible account, visit cph.org/podcast and listen to our Seeds of Faith podcast each week.**

## Lesson 2
# God Creates Adam and Eve
### Genesis 1:26–2:25

## Get Ready
### Before Class

- Copy Student Page 2 for each person.

- For **Opening**, get a stopwatch or clock, newsprint, masking tape, and markers. Hang up a newsprint sheet.

- For **God Speaks**, preview the Lesson 2 YouTube video in the Old Testament 1 High School playlist at **bit.ly/1knXwnU**. To use it, get equipment ready (e.g., computer, tablet, Internet connection) and cue the video.

  Get Bibles, the Timeline Poster, newsprint, markers, masking tape, and crayons.

- For **We Live**, hang up a sheet of newsprint. Use students' newsprint sheets from God Speaks.

# 1 Opening (10 minutes)

### Invisible Qualities

Write "invisible" at the top of your newsprint sheet. Recruit a volunteer to run the stopwatch.

**Say** Let's brainstorm as many *invisible* things as we can in two minutes. Brainstorming means we don't judge responses, such as saying something isn't true. We just list them. Stopwatch holder, tell us when to go.

Write items students mention on the sheet, stopping at two minutes. They'll probably run out of ideas early. Step back and look at the list.

**Ask** What observations can we make about our list? Let students respond.

If the word *God* is on the list, put a star by it. If it is not, add it.

Hand out Student Page 2 copies and ask a volunteer to read **Romans 1:20** at the top of the page. Continue adding to the list.

**What qualities of God are invisible?** His eternal power and divine nature. God is a Spirit (John 4:24; 2 Corinthians 3:17).

**Where do God's qualities show?** In the things He made, in creation

**What other qualities of God are invisible?** God's presence (even in the Lord's Supper), power, wisdom, love, protection, and so on

If students brainstormed invisible qualities of people, circle them.

**What things about people are invisible?** Personality, sense of humor, ideas, thoughts, cellular structure, undiagnosed disease, DNA, and so on.

If students do not mention it, add *sin* to the list. If they did, underline it.

**Say** We're born in sin and cannot stop sinning. We don't do the things we want to do. In fact, we do the very things we hate.

Ask someone to read **Colossians 1:13–15** (Student Page).

**Ask** What did God do to help us with our sin dilemma? He rescued us from the dominion of darkness and transferred us to the kingdom of His Son, who paid the price for our sin and forgives us.

**What words describe Jesus, God's Son?** Beloved, image of the invisible God

**Say** We'll discover more about God's image today.

**Pray** Heavenly Father, You give us all good gifts, even though we do not deserve them. Especially today, we thank You for Your invisible gifts to us, especially Your love, mercy, and saving grace in Christ Jesus. Amen.

# 2 God Speaks (32 minutes)

## Key Point

God has made us in His image, provides all things for our good, and makes us rulers over the earth and everything in it.

## Creating Humans

**Ask** **What in creation amazes you?** Answers vary.

If you do not show the video, continue with the next "Say" statement.

Show the Lesson 2 YouTube video, "Making the Solar System" (3:25), in the Old Testament 1 High School playlist at **bit.ly/1knXwnU**.

**Ask** **What amazes you about the scale model of our solar system?** Answers vary and may include the small sizes used to represent the sun and planets and the space needed to make the scale model.

**Considering these things, what might you infer about the Creator?** Answers vary and may include that God is "big" and beyond our imagination. Our solar system is one of billions. Our organized and systematic solar system shows God's attention to intricate details.

**Say** **Humans are God's most amazing creation. Our lesson today digs into two accounts about the creation of people.**

Show the Timeline Poster to demonstrate the lesson context.

Return to the Student Page and read the directions: **Read Genesis 1:26–31 or 2:5–7. List (1) words used for the Creator, (2) the being(s) created, (3) how it happened, and (4) supplies and patterns used.**

*Digs into God's Word*

Divide students into groups of two to four people. Assign **Genesis 1:26–31** or **2:5–7** to each. If you have only a few students, assign a reference to each person.

Point out the newsprint and markers. Give students about ten minutes to read their verses and list the four parts, shown below. As students work, help as needed and review questions to prepare for discussion.

|  | Genesis 1:26–31 | Genesis 2:5–7 |
|---|---|---|
| **1. Words used for the Creator** | God; Us; Our; His; He; I | "Lord God" |
| **2. Being(s) created** | humans, male and female | man (woman not created until 2:18–25) |
| **3. How it happened** | God created (v. 27) | Lord God formed man of dust from the ground, breathed into his nostrils the breath of life, and man became a living creature |
| **4. Supplies/patterns used** | God's image, after God's likeness (v. 26); God's own image, male and female (v. 27) | man of dust formed from the ground, breath of life (v. 7) |

## Debriefing

When time elapses, gather everyone together and have groups hang up their drawings. Ask **Genesis 1** groups to present their drawings first; then, **Genesis 2** groups follow. Ask clarifying questions to make sure content is presented.

## Pronunciations

Assyria: ah SEER ee ah
Cush: kush
Euphrates:
     you FRAY tease
Gihon: GIH hon
Havilah: HAV uh luh
Pishon : PEE shawn
Tigris: TIE gris

## Key Point

God has made us in His image, provides all things for our good, and makes us rulers over the earth and everything in it.

**Goes to the Heart**

## Digging Deeper

Continue with questions on the Student Page.

**Ask** **What observations can we make about these two creation accounts?** Let students share ideas. Each provides information about the same story. They complement, not conflict. The first shows the big picture, the second details.

**Identify the big picture of God creating humans in Genesis 1.** God made humans last as part of creating the entire universe. He created male and female in His image, after His likeness.

**What commands did God give people in Genesis 1?** Be fruitful and multiply, fill the earth and subdue it, have dominion over all other creatures (v. 28). Humans and all other creatures should eat plants (vv. 29–30).

**Look for details in Genesis 2. God had not yet sent rain. How did He water the earth?** A mist went up from the ground (2:6).

**Since a mist came from the ground, from what did God make man?** Mud. *Yatsar*, the Hebrew word for "formed," is related to the word for "potter," one who forms pots with wet clay (*TLSB*, p. 16; 2:7 note).

**What evidence shows that humans are made from dust?** After death, our bodies decay and return to dust.

**Moses used two different names for God in Genesis 1 and 2.** *Elohim*, **the plural noun for "God" in Genesis 1, means "the strong one." Why does this fit chapter 1?** Our strong, powerful God created the universe. The plural noun shows evidence of the Trinity. All three persons of the Godhead were present.

Jews reject the Trinity, just as they reject Jesus. They say the plural noun "Us" is used in the same way royalty say "we" instead of "I."

Christians agree there is one God but accept Jesus as the Savior and the Trinity as an explanation for who God is. The doctrine of the Trinity is one major dividing line between Christians and non-Christian religions that reject it, such as Mormons, Jehovah's Witnesses, and Muslims.

**Genesis 2 uses "Lord God," the Hebrew word** *Yahweh*, **which is the name God revealed to Moses from the burning bush. It means "I AM WHO I AM" and indicates His eternal nature. It shows God's grace, mercy, and compassion in the covenant relationship with His people. How is this name appropriate for Genesis 2?** God's personal relationship with man started at creation with the intimate way He created people.

## Providing Purpose

Ask volunteers to read sections of **Genesis 2:8–25** and discuss these questions.

**8–9** **What special trees did God plant in the garden?** The tree of life and the tree of the knowledge of good and evil

**10–15** **Why did God put the man in the garden?** To work and keep it

**What does this say about work?** Work is a good gift from God, not a curse that came after man sinned. God wants us to have purposeful work and lives. As Christians, all our work and service honors God. If anyone is unwilling to work, don't let him eat (2 Thessalonians 3:10).

**Does this change your view of work? If so, how?** Answers vary.

**16–17** **What did God tell the man about the two special trees?** He could eat from any tree in the garden except the tree of the knowledge of good and evil. If he ate fruit from that tree, he would die.

**18–20** **Why did God bring the animals to man?** It wasn't good for man to be alone. God wanted him to have a helper. He let the man name the animals.

**21–25** **When the man did not find a suitable animal helper, what did God do?** He created woman.

**How did God create woman?** He put Adam to sleep, took a rib, and made her. Woman was made from the same stuff as Adam (dust) and in God's image.

**How does this show the close relationship between man and woman?** The first woman was made out of man; since then, humans are knit together in women's wombs (Psalm 139:13) and come out of them.

**Say** **Luther says that God established the household when He created Eve. This act made Adam a husband and joined to him a wife who would be his complement.**

# 3 We Live (15 minutes)

## Uniquely Made

These questions are not on the Student Page, but the Bible references are.

**Ask** **What makes people different from animals?** Direct students to look at their newsprint sheets from God Speaks to find one thing in each reading. Genesis 1:27 says God made man in His image (likeness). Genesis 2:7 says God breathed the breath of life into man.

**Say** **The Hebrew word *tselem*, translated as "image," means more than physical resemblance. Adam reflected God's character and virtues. He was God's representative in the world and His steward of the earth, as commanded in 1:28** (*TLSB*, p. 14; 1:26 note)**.**

**What characteristics and virtues of God did humans made in His image have?** They reflected God's qualities, such as His perfection, sinlessness, creativity, and contentedness, and they had no fear of death since they ate from the tree of life. Most of all, God gave them the will and knowledge to please Him.

**What did God's breath give people?** Life, an eternal soul

**Humans still have souls. Do we still have the image of God?** No and yes.

No, when sin came into the world "the will and intellect lost the ability to know and please God" (*Luther's Small Catechism with Explanation*, Question 107). As sinners, we rebel against God; we are His enemies (Romans 5:10) and cannot know Him unless the Spirit works through God's Word and Sacraments to give us faith (1 Corinthians 12:3).

Yes, God's image is being restored in Christians. As the Spirit works in us through God's Word, we become more like Jesus, the image of God. On this side of heaven, we will always fight our sinful nature and won't be fully remade into the image of Christ until we live with Him forever.

## Faith in Action

Encourage students to cut out and post one or more of the Bible verses from We Live in a place they see every day, such as a bathroom mirror, closet door, or dash of a car.

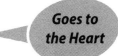

*Goes to the Heart*

Lesson 2

## Key Point

God has made us in His image, provides all things for our good, and makes us rulers over the earth and everything in it.

**How do we work with the Spirit as He conforms us to the image of Christ?**
Ask volunteers to read **Romans 8:29; Colossians 2:12–13; Ephesians 4:22–24; 1 Corinthians 6:19–20; Philippians 2:13** (on Student Page). Hang up a sheet of newsprint to record key phrases or ideas as words or symbols.

- The Spirit works to conform us to the image of His Son (Romans 8:29).

- In Baptism, we were buried and raised with Jesus through faith. Although dead in sin, God made us alive and forgave our sins (Colossians 2:12–13).

- God's Spirit works in us (through Word and Sacrament) to help us put off the old self (confess our sins and receive forgiveness) and "put on the new self, created after the likeness of God in true righteousness and holiness" (Ephesians 4:24).

- The Holy Spirit lives in us and renews us by the Gospel now. We honor God (give glory) when we confess faith in Him by praising Him (*TLSB*, p. 1230; Jeremiah 13:16 note).

- We will continue to struggle with sin on this side of heaven. God will not finish conforming us to Christ's image until we die and live with Him.

- Saved in Christ, we cooperate with the Spirit. We take comfort knowing God works in us to will and work to please Him. It's not all up to us. The Spirit helps. Made in God's image, Adam and Eve willed and worked to please God.

**Say** Adam and Eve were created in God's image and lived according to God's will, until they sinned. We clearly see sin in ourselves and the world. We need a Savior. The Good News is that God provided one through His Son. His love and forgiveness restore our right relationship with God.

 **4 Closing** (3 minutes)

Ask students to write a few words or to draw a symbol on their page that reminds them of God's work in them and helps them live as Christians.

Ask volunteers to share their responses. Thank those who do.

Close by confessing the Apostles' Creed or saying the Lord's Prayer.

Growing in CHRIST

# Lesson 2
# God creates Adam and Eve
Genesis 1:26–2:25

> **Romans 1:20:** [God's] invisible attributes, namely, His eternal power and divine nature, have been clearly perceived, ever since the creation of the world, in the things that have been made.
>
> **Colossians 1:13–15:** [God] has delivered us from the domain of darkness and transferred us to the kingdom of His beloved Son, in whom we have redemption, the forgiveness of sins. He is the image of the invisible God.

## Creating humans

**Directions:** Read **Genesis 1:26–31** or **2:5–7**. List (1) words used for the Creator, (2) the being(s) created, (3) how it happened, (4) and supplies and patterns used.

## Digging deeper

- What observations can we make about these two creation accounts?
- Identify the big picture of God creating humans in **Genesis 1**.
- What commands did God give people in **Genesis 1**?
- Look for details in **Genesis 2**. God had not yet sent rain. How did He water the earth?
- Since a mist came from the ground, from what did God make man?
- What evidence shows that humans are made from dust?
- Moses used two different names for God in Genesis 1 and 2. *Elohim*, the plural noun for "God" in **Genesis 1**, means "the strong one." Why does this fit chapter 1?
- **Genesis 2** uses "Lord God," the Hebrew word *Yahweh*, which is the name God revealed to Moses from the burning bush. It means "I AM WHO I AM" and indicates His eternal nature. It shows God's grace, mercy, and compassion in the covenant relationship with His people. How is this name appropriate for chapter 2?

## Providing purpose

Read **Genesis 2:8–25**.
- What special trees did God plant in the garden?
- Why did God put the man in the garden?
- What does this say about work?
- Does this change your view of work? If so, how?
- What did God tell the man about the two special trees?
- Why did God bring the animals to man?
- When the man did not find a suitable animal helper, what did God do?
- How did God create woman?
- How does this show the close relationship between man and woman?

## Uniquely made

**Romans 8:29:** For those whom He foreknew He also predestined to be conformed to the image of His Son, in order that He might be the firstborn among many brothers.

**Colossians 2:12–13:** Having been buried with Him in baptism, in which you were also raised with Him through faith in the powerful working of God, who raised Him from the dead. And you, who were dead in your trespasses and the uncircumcision of your flesh, God made alive together with him, having forgiven us all our trespasses.

**Ephesians 4:22–24:** Put off your old self, which belongs to your former manner of life and is corrupt through deceitful desires, and to be renewed in the spirit of your minds, and to put on the new self, created after the likeness of God in true righteousness and holiness.

**1 Corinthians 6:19–20:** Do you not know that your body is a temple of the Holy Spirit within you, whom you have from God? You are not your own, for you were bought with a price. So glorify God in your body.

**Philippians 2:13:** It is God who works in you, both to will and to work for his good pleasure.

# Preparing the Lesson

## Sin Enters the World

Genesis 3

## Key Point

Through Adam, sin spreads to all people. Through Christ, God offers forgiveness to all people.

## Law/Gospel

Because I sin, I will die. **God sent His Son, Jesus, to crush sin, death, and the devil, and through Him, God forgives my sins and gives me eternal life.**

## Context

It appears that angels were created before the earth and that some rebelled during that time (Job 38:4–7; 2 Peter 2:4). St. Augustine reasoned that the fall of some angels must have occurred at the instant of their creation, when they chose to look to self instead of to God; otherwise, they would have known that God's service is infinitely sweeter than self-service. We say that those angels who know the sweetness of serving God are confirmed in grace and will never fall away.

Evil is not part of the created world; it arises from disordered love. In Eve's case, she placed the love of knowledge (a good thing) over obedience (a better thing).

## Commentary

The serpent, or snake, is identified as Satan ("accuser") in Revelation 12:9. He is "crafty," which implies manipulation to suit self, as opposed to being wise, which implies conforming self to God's truth. The serpent begins with an implied lie: "Did God actually say . . . ?" (Genesis 3:1). He attacks Eve's faith, her confidence in what God had said. He continues with a bald-faced lie: "You will not surely die. . . . Your eyes will be opened, and you will be like God" (vv. 4–5).

Eve chooses to believe the serpent rather than God. Sin is breaking the Law (1 John 3:4) or disobeying God, but its roots lie in the lack of faith in what God has said. Characteristically, Satan leads us from doubt of God's Law into sin; then he leads us, in our guilt, to doubt God's Gospel and to despair.

Adam trusts his wife more than God's Word, and so he follows her into sin. Now they "know" (experience) the difference between good and evil. Feeling self-conscious and ashamed, they cover themselves. The sound of God walking in the cool of the day is no longer welcome but is a cause of dread. Confronted with guilt, Adam blames God and Eve: "the woman whom You gave to be with me" (Genesis 3:12). Eve blames the serpent.

God's curse of the serpent is good news for the descendants of Adam. Genesis 3:15 is known as the protoevangel, or "first Gospel." The woman's Seed would be victorious, crushing the head of the serpent despite being wounded in the process. The tree of the knowledge of good and evil became the instrument of condemnation; the tree of the cross would become the instrument of salvation.

God's judgment on Eve takes the form of a "cross" laid on marriage. Now this gift will entail the pain of childbearing, and the husband's rule will be experienced as oppression. The judgment on Adam is the frustration and drudgery of work, ending in the return to dust through physical death.

God makes garments of skins for Adam and Eve (v. 21); animals had to die. Thereafter, human life, both physical and spiritual, is sustained by the death or sacrifice of animals. The closing judgment against both Adam and Eve is for them to be driven from Eden with its tree of (eternal) life. What they were made for is closed off to them and their descendants. Mankind has lost the image of God until it is restored in Christ, the new Adam.

**To hear an in-depth discussion of this Bible account, visit cph.org/podcast and listen to our Seeds of Faith podcast each week.**

## Lesson 3

# Sin Enters the World

Genesis 3

- Copy Student Page 3 for each person.

- For **Opening**, preview the Lesson 3 YouTube video in the Old Testament 1 High School playlist at **bit.ly/1knXwnU**. To use it, get equipment ready (e.g., computer, tablet, Internet connection) and cue the video.

- For **God Speaks**, get Bibles, the Timeline Poster, newsprint, markers, pencils, and masking tape.

- For **We Live**, collect items for the activity, such as cotton balls, tissues, stickers, pennies, toothpicks, adhesive bandages, erasers, candy kisses, Lifesaver candies, and rubber bands. You may have two or three of the same item.

## ① Opening (10 minutes)

### Filled or Empty

**Ask**  **Are you filled or empty?** Ask students to reply one by one; when each one does, ask how he or she decided. **Did you just eat? Are you hungry? Are you excited about a new friendship or challenge? Did you just come from worship? Did you recently take Holy Communion?**

If you do not watch the video, adapt the questions to talk about what fills us up.

**Say**  **Let's watch this video to get a little more perspective.**

Show the Lesson 3 YouTube video, "Filled" (2:55), in the Old Testament 1 High School playlist at **bit.ly/1knXwnU**.

**Ask**  **Who wants to change their answer to the question?**

**What kind of things that the man mentioned also fill you up, at least for a while?** Let students share as they feel comfortable. Ask individuals to respond.

**True or untrue for you? "What I want, I can have it. With the touch of a button, at the drop of a hat, the world is at my fingertips."** Answers vary.

**How would you describe these words by the man: "No wonder I don't need God. I'm already full"?** Answers vary and may include sad, because he fills up on junk when he needs a relationship with God; happy, because he's content.

**What Bible account came to mind when the man said, "All I have to do is convince myself that it's good to eat and desirable for food. Then it's just a matter of plucking my choice fruit from the tree"?** The words echo Genesis 3 about the fall of man, which we study today.

**Pray**  **Dear Jesus, You came to the world to live the life we could not live. You gave Yourself up for sinners, who turn against You and fill themselves up with junk. Thank You for being the Second Adam, paying for our sins, and making us right with God. Shape and mold us to Your image. Amen.**

## ② God Speaks (32 minutes)

### Paradise Lost

**Say**  **I am going to read some thoughts. If you have had thoughts like these, put your thumb up. If not, put your thumb down.**

- **God seems to love some people more than others.**

**Growing in CHRIST.**

Key Point
Through Adam, sin spreads to all people. Through Christ, God offers forgiveness to all people.

- ▨ **Some people always seem to win and get what they want.**
- ▨ **if I behave and go to church, God should give me everything I want.**
- ▨ **Sometimes, I wonder if God is real.**
- ▨ **Why did my loved one die?**
- ▨ **When is God going to tell me what to do with my life?**
- ▨ **Is everything in the Bible true?**

**Say**   **No matter how you voted, you need to know that everyone has doubts from time to time. What should we do when we doubt?** We need to turn to God's Word and pray for the Spirit's guidance. We can talk to Christian friends, our parents, and our pastor or other church workers. We can know it's okay to wonder and let God speak to us through His Word and Sacraments.

**Builds Relationships**

**Say**   **Let's turn to God's Word to discuss the fall into sin.**

Hand out Bibles and copies of Student Page 3. Divide into groups of two to five people. Let groups choose a character to represent: the serpent, Eve, Adam, or God. If you have fewer students, assign a role to each or take one yourself.

Read together **Genesis 2:16–17**, God's command about the tree (Student Page).

**Say**   **As we read Genesis 3 aloud together, consider the event from your character's viewpoint. Jot notes about what your character wanted, did, and doubted. What resulted from your character's behavior?**

Recruit volunteers to read five parts in **Genesis 3**—the serpent, Eve, Adam, God, and narrator—as others read along.

**Digs into God's Word**

**Say**   **Now, each group draw a picture of your character and at least one speech bubble that tells the character's wants, efforts, doubts, and results.**

Point out supplies, such as newsprint, markers, and pencils. Tell groups they have ten minutes to work. Help as needed and review questions to prepare for discussion.

## Serpent
- ▨ **Wants:** Desired to lead humans into sin, separate them from God, and spite God.
- ▨ **Efforts:** A fallen angel, the devil possessed the snake, or appeared in its form (*TLSB*, p. 17; 3:1 note). Crafty, he lied to Eve and sowed doubts about God's Word (you won't die; God doesn't mean it) and God's desires for her (God doesn't want you to know as much as Him; eat the fruit to see more, be like Him, and be wise).
- ▨ **Doubts:** Didn't think God would hurt him, despite losing an earlier battle with God and being thrown out of heaven. He pursued Eve and Adam with hatred for the Lord.
- ▨ **Results:** (1) Success. Eve rejected God's Word, and humans disobeyed and lost the image of God, which includes the knowledge of God and the will to please Him. (2) Busted, cursed. The snake would slither on its belly and eat dust. People would hate snakes, and visa versa. The devil would lose a battle with Eve's offspring, giving a bruised heel but receiving a bruised head.

## Eve
- ▨ **Wants:** Even though Eve was made in God's image and already like Him, knowing only good, not evil, she wanted more. The devil made her doubt God's Word. Hungry, she believed his lies.
- ▨ **Efforts:** Eve added to God's command ("neither shall you touch it"). Sin already snared her. One untruth led to another sin.

■ **Doubts:** Didn't believe God's Word, warning, and will for her (not to know evil).

■ **Results:** When doubt opened the door, Eve noticed that the fruit looked tasty and thought it would make her wise. She ate and gave it to Adam. Eyes opened, she saw nakedness, made clothes, and hid from God. She blamed the serpent. She would have great pain in pregnancy and birth. She will desire her husband; he will rule over her.

### Adam

■ **Wants:** He wishes to be with Eve and to satiate his hunger.

■ **Efforts:** He ate the fruit Eve gave him.

■ **Doubts:** He didn't trust God's intentions. Since he was present and ate the fruit, Adam also may have believed the serpent's lies.

■ **Results.** Eyes opened, he saw nakedness, made clothes, and hid from God. He blamed Eve. The ground was cursed to make work more difficult. He would die and return to dust.

### God

■ **Wants:** His desire was to enjoy and bless perfect humans, made in His likeness, as they lived in and tended the garden He made for them.

■ **Effort:** God came to see Adam and Eve, making His presence known in the Garden.

■ **Doubts:** Absolutely none.

■ **Results:** Asked the humans why they were hiding, even though He knew why: they had eaten the forbidden fruit. Cursed the snake/devil; said he would suffer fatal injuries from Eve's offspring, the promised Messiah. Gave Eve and Adam the promised consequences (death) and more. Compassionately made animal-skin clothing for Adam and Eve. Sent humans out of the Garden so they couldn't eat from the tree of life and live forever in sin. Set a cherubim to guard the way.

## Debriefing

When time elapses, bring everyone together and ask them to hang up pictures. Let serpent groups show their pictures and speech bubbles. If needed, ask questions to make key points. Continue with the other characters in the same way.

Then continue with these questions (not on the Student Page).

**Ask** **How did the woman react when the serpent spoke to her?** Eve was neither surprised nor afraid. Temptation disguised itself beautifully. If this were not so, Eve would not have talked with it so calmly.

**How was the world different before sin?** There was no death, decay, fear, or distrust. Humans lived with God and the animals in perfect harmony.

**The Hebrew word for "crafty" is almost identical to the word for "naked." Why is this amazing but true fact important?** Before sin entered the world, God's creation was perfect; embarrassment and shame didn't exist. The human body, the crown of God's creation, was perfect and there was no need to cover it up. The craftiness of the serpent allowed the devil to work through this creature to bring about Adam and Eve's shame when they knew they were naked.

**Made in God's image, Adam and Eve had God's Law in their hearts** (Jeremiah 31:31–34), **yet they chose to disobey. We often make this choice too. Name a time when you could have not done something, but you did it anyway.**

Share an example of your own. Encourage students to share.

**How did God care for Adam and Eve eternally, even though they turned away from Him?** In Genesis 3:15, God promised the Savior, the One who would bruise the devil's head. This is the first Gospel promise in Scripture. The promised Savior is Christ. The devil bruised the heel of Eve's offspring when He died on Good Friday, but He crushed the devil's head when He rose from the dead.

**How does God care for us, despite our sin and disobedience?** Students may list many ways God cares for us, as we ask for in the Lord's Prayer as "daily bread." This includes "everything that has to do with the support and needs of the body" (Small Catechism, Fourth Petition).

Best of all, in Christ, God provided His Son as our Savior. Without sin, yet crucified for our sin, Jesus paid the debt of all sinners for all time. Believers receive His forgiveness of sins and the promise of eternal life. Because He rose from the dead, we, too, will live. We receive these gifts from Jesus in Baptism, Holy Communion, and by hearing and learning God's Word.

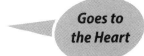

*Goes to the Heart*

## 3 We Live (15 minutes)

### Resisting Temptation

Put the objects you brought in the center of your group: cotton balls, tissues, stickers, pennies, toothpicks, bandages, erasers, candy kisses, and so on.

Ask volunteers to read the Bible verses from the right column of the Student Page: **Hebrews 2:14; 1 John 3:8; 1 Corinthians 10:13; Hebrews 2:18.**

**Ask** **What comfort and power does God give us in these verses?** Let students share ideas. Jesus defeated the devil for us. God will not let us be tempted beyond our ability and will provide a way of escape so we can endure it. Because Jesus suffered when tempted, He can help us when we are tempted.

**Say** **Pick an object for yourself and one to give a friend as encouragement to resist temptation. For example, the tissue might remind you to dry your tears and trust Jesus to forgive you and help you.**

*Active Learning*

Once all have chosen, ask students to take turns telling what one item means to them. A toothpick might remind us to "pick out" good qualities in others instead of looking for negatives. An eraser might remind us that everyone makes mistakes and that we have forgiveness of sins in Christ Jesus.

**Say** **We are infected with sin, but because of Christ's work, our sins are forgiven. God loves us and provides for us. God works through His Word and Sacraments to create and maintain our faith and give us the hope of "going home" to paradise with Him.**

### Faith in Action
Encourage students to give the item they picked for a friend to one of their friends with the explanation they shared in class.

## 4 Closing (3 minutes)

**Say** **Name one thing you learned that you can tell someone else.** Thank students who share.

Close by saying Luther's Morning Prayer together (Student Page).

# Lesson 3
# Sin enters the world
Genesis 3

## Paradise lost

**Genesis 2:16–17:** And the LORD God commanded the man, saying, "You may surely eat of every tree of the garden, but of the tree of the knowledge of good and evil you shall not eat, for in the day that you eat of it you shall surely die."

**Directions:** Choose a character: serpent, Eve, Adam, or God. Identify these items for your character from **Genesis 3**.

**Wants**

**Efforts**

**Doubts**

**Results**

Draw a picture (on separate paper) of your character with at least one speech bubble that tells his or her wants, efforts, doubts, and results.

## Resisting temptation

**Hebrews 2:14:** Since therefore the children share in flesh and blood, [Jesus] Himself likewise partook of the same things, that through death He might destroy the one who has the power of death, that is, the devil.

**1 John 3:8:** The reason the Son of God appeared was to destroy the works of the devil.

**1 Corinthians 10:13:** No temptation has overtaken you that is not common to man. God is faithful, and He will not let you be tempted beyond your ability, but with the temptation He will also provide the way of escape, that you may be able to endure it.

**Hebrews 2:18:** For because [Jesus] Himself has suffered when tempted, He is able to help those who are being tempted.

## Luther's Morning Prayer

I thank You, my heavenly Father, through Jesus Christ, Your dear Son, that You have kept me this night from all harm and danger; and I pray that You would keep me this day also from sin and every evil, that all my doings and life may please You.

For into Your hands I commend myself, my body and soul, and all things. Let Your holy angel be with me, that the evil foe may have no power over me. Amen.

# Preparing the Lesson

## Cain and Abel

Genesis 4:1–16

## Key Point

Even though Cain sinned, God still loved and preserved him. Even though we sin, God, in Christ, still loves and preserves us.

## Law/Gospel

I sin when I trust myself or my own deeds to please God. **God loves me and sent His Son, Jesus, to be the perfect sacrifice for my sin. Through faith in Him, I am marked as God's child and receive His gifts of forgiveness, life, and salvation.**

## Context

The biblical chapter divisions with which we are familiar were not added until the completed Scriptures were already one thousand years old. Neither they nor the chapter headings added by modern editors are part of the inspired Word. Genesis 4 is often designated as being about Cain and Abel. The chapter is really about Adam, now cursed by sin.

Adam and Eve did not physically die the same day they first sinned; they lived on, raised children, had hopes dashed, and experienced the death of one child at the hand of another.

## Commentary

Eve's words in Genesis 4:1 could be translated "I have brought forth a man, the Lord." Some scholars have seen this as her expectation that Cain was the one to crush the serpent. If so, these hopes would be dashed.

The offering made by Abel, the shepherd, proved acceptable to God, while that of Cain, the farmer, did not. Hebrews 11:4 states that Abel made the acceptable offering by faith. Cain's feelings of disappointment and jealousy boiled over into a premeditated act of murder. Ironically, his desire to please God on one level led to this sinful impulse.

Abel, the innocent shepherd whose offering was accepted by God, was killed for it. In this way, Abel was a type (foreshadowing) of Christ. Abel is the first example of the persecution of the faithful—what St. Augustine called the war waged by the city of man on the city of God.

God confronts Cain, who responds with a lie, followed by this impudent question: "Am I my brother's keeper?" (Genesis 4:9). The implied answer is yes.

As Adam was cursed for his sin, so Cain is also cursed; however, the mark of Cain is actually a sign of mercy proclaiming an end to vengeance. Like other laws of God, it protects people from the coarse outbursts of sin. Cain's line of descendants does not produce the promised Seed—that comes through Seth, who is born later—and, after a brief genealogy, Scripture tells us no more about Cain.

**To hear an in-depth discussion of this Bible account, visit cph.org/podcast and listen to our Seeds of Faith podcast each week.**

# Cain and Abel

Genesis 4:1–16

## Get Ready
### Before Class

- Copy Student Page 4 for each person.

- For **Opening**, preview the Lesson 4 YouTube video in the Old Testament 1 High School playlist at **bit.ly/1knXwnU**. To use it, get equipment ready (e.g., computer, tablet, Internet connection) and cue the video.

- For **God Speaks**, get Bibles, the Timeline Poster, newsprint, masking tape, and markers.

  Cut out a large newsprint heart and trace around it on another sheet of newsprint. Hang up the newsprint heart. Set the cutout heart out of sight to use later.

## ① Opening (10 minutes)

### Getting into It

**Say** Let's do a quick activity to get us thinking.

Ask everyone to get up and stand in an open area.

**Say** Imagine a straight line from wall to wall. I'll give you two choices. Stand somewhere on the line to show your answer. If you like both, stand in the middle. If you like one better than the other, stand closer to that end.

Answer questions; then begin posing choices. As you do, point to an end for each choice. Let students vote with their feet. After each vote, pause briefly to ask a student or two to explain their answers.

**Ask** Which do you like best—winter or spring? summer or fall? football or volleyball? baseball or softball?

Whom do you argue with more—a friend or a neighbor? your mom or your dad? teachers or other students? a brother or a sister?

What makes it most difficult for you to reconcile conflicts— being right or being wrong? your pride or your lack of confidence? anger or hurt? fear of punishment or the need to win?

If you do not use the video, skip to the second "Say" statement.

**Say** Pick out the conflict and the consequences in this video.

Show the Lesson 4 YouTube video, "Jedi Kittens Strike Back," (0:51) in the Old Testament 1 High School playlist at **bit.ly/1knXwnU**.

**Ask** Whom was the conflict between? How did it resolve? What were the consequences? Kittens fought in Star Wars jets and then with lasers. They both crashed. Their owner grounded them and told them to clean up.

How does this silly video demonstrate what often happens in households? Let willing students share. As they do, you might ask, **Do you argue with siblings? Do you talk things out? Does the person who stops the conflict or hands out consequences always understand the skirmish?**

**Say** We'll find out about a family conflict today.

**Pray** Lord God, we want to do Your will, but instead we argue, fight, and sin. Thank You for rescuing us through the life, death, and resurrection of Your Son, Christ. Keep us in this one true faith. In Jesus' name we pray. Amen.

# ② **God Speaks** (32 minutes)

## Heart-to-Heart

Stand near the newsprint with the large heart, as specified in Get Ready.

**Say** **Thoughts come from our minds. What comes from our hearts?** Write comments inside the heart (e.g., emotions, faith, love).

Hand out copies of Student Page 4. Ask a volunteer to read **Mark 7:21–22** (on Student Page). As he or she does, in a different ink color, write what Jesus said comes from the heart inside the newsprint heart (evil thoughts and so on).

**Ask** **How are the things Jesus listed alike or different from what we listed?** Help students know that our hearts are sinful. Write across the heart: *old heart*.

**How do we show that we inherited the disease of sin?** We can't stop sinning or make sin go away by ourselves. It's stuck to us like the stickiest tar.

Use another marker to color the whole heart. You will use it again in **We Live**.

**Say** **Let's dig into Scripture to find out more.**

## Brother versus Brother

Show the Timeline Poster to demonstrate the lesson context.

Divide into groups of two to five people. Assign each group to illustrate Cain or Abel as they read and discuss **Genesis 4:1–16**.

If you choose to keep your group together, hang up two sheets of newsprint and make profiles of Cain and Abel together.

Point out the newsprint and markers. Tell groups they have twenty minutes to discuss all the questions and draw their pictures. As students work, help as needed and review questions to prepare for discussion.

**1–2** **Draw a large cookie-cutter-type outline of a person. Add details from these verses for your assigned brother, Cain or Abel.** Cain, the firstborn, worked as a farmer. Abel, born second, shepherd.

*Cain* **sounds similar to the Hebrew phrase "I have gotten." Some scholars, including Martin Luther, think Eve believed she birthed the promised offspring who would defeat the devil and regain paradise (Genesis 3:15). If so, how do you think Adam and Eve treated Cain? Show this on your drawing of Cain.** Luther said, "without a doubt Cain was very highly regarded and considered the favorite" (AE 1:243). Their names and occupations show this. Adam trained his favorite son to do his work. Abel cared for the flock.

**In Hebrew,** *Abel* **means "breath or vapor," implying something temporary. Show this on your drawing of Abel.** Answers vary.

**3–7** **The Hebrew word translated as** *had regard* **means "looked at" or "paid attention to." Genesis does not say why God accepted Abel's sacrifice but not Cain's, so we let Scripture interpret Scripture. Read 1 John 3:12, Hosea 6:6, 1 Samuel 16:7, and James 4:6** (Student Page) **to find out why. Show these things on your drawings.** Cain was evil; Abel was made righteous by faith. Cain didn't trust God or worship Him with a true heart; Abel did. God wants our love, not begrudging sacrifices. The Lord looks at hearts, not appearance.

## Key Point

Even though Cain sinned, God still loved and preserved him. Even though we sin, God in Christ still loves and preserves us.

*Digs into God's Word*

Cain acted proud and arrogant. Abel was humble, and God counted him as righteous because he trusted Him. This faith was a gift Abel received from God; he did nothing to receive it. We cannot earn God's favor either. He renders us righteous through faith in Christ Jesus, just as Old Testament believers trusted God's promises to send the Savior offspring.

Cain rejected this gift and trusted other things instead—perhaps his status in the family, his reputation, or his parents' faith.

Luther said, "So the fault lay not in the materials which were offered but in the person of him who brought the offering. The faith of the individual was the weight which added value to Abel's offering" (AE 1:251).

**How did Cain react to God's displeasure? Show Cain's reaction and your ideas on your drawing.** Cain became angry, and his face fell. This means he felt disappointed, embarrassed, or shamed.

**God spoke Law to show Cain his sin so he would repent and come back to God. What did God warn Cain about?** Sin was ready to pounce on him. Jealousy and anger fester and lead to dangerous actions. God warned Cain to stop and adjust his thinking and attitudes before he sinned more egregiously.

**8–16** **How did Cain act out his emotions?** He let frustration, anger, envy, and rejection boil over into a murderous fury at his brother.

**What kind of criminal charge could we bring against Cain today?** Cain asked Abel to come into the field with him. He planned to take Abel's life. Today, this is evidence of premeditated, or first-degree, murder.

**God knew where Abel was when He asked Cain where his brother was. Why did He ask?** He gave Cain a chance to admit his sin and seek God's forgiveness. **What did Cain do?** He lied.

**What consequences did God give Cain for this sin?** God cursed Cain so the ground would no longer provide his living. He would wander the earth.

**How did Cain react? What does this show was in Cain's heart? Show this on your drawing of Cain.** Cain whined, felt sorry for himself, and showed a lack of repentance and a shirking of responsibility. He blamed God and did not repent. He worried that other siblings would take his life.

Cain expected the worst, saying he would be separated from God. God did not say this, and it was not true. God continued to care for Cain as He did for Adam and Eve. Cain's heart was filled with a mixture of self-pity, emotions, and sin.

**How did God show mercy to Cain? Show this on your drawing of Cain.** God put a mark on Cain that told others to leave him alone. We don't know where it was, but it must have been easily visible. God said He would take sevenfold vengeance on anyone who hurt Cain. He did not abandon Cain or separate from him, but He continued to care for him.

## Debriefing

When time elapses, call groups back and hang up drawings. Starting with Abel groups, give each a short time to explain what they drew. Then continue with Cain groups. Discuss select questions that were not covered in presentations, especially the question about why God accepted Abel's offering but not Cain's.

# 3 We Live (15 minutes)

## A True Heart, A Pure Heart

Scriptures are on the Student Page, but questions are not.

Ask a volunteer to read **John 14:6** (Student Page).

**Ask** **What do we have in common with Cain and Abel?** We were born in sin and cannot escape it without God's help. We need a Savior.

**Say** **The Book of Hebrews tells how Jesus fulfilled the Old Testament sacrificial system. A curtain separated the Most Holy Place from the rest of the temple. The high priest went in the Most Holy Place once a year on the Day of Atonement to sprinkle the blood of a sacrificed lamb. When Christ died, this heavily embroidered curtain split from top to bottom** (Luke 23:45)**.**

Ask volunteers to read **Hebrews 10:19–22** and **12:22, 24** (Student Page). As they do, tape the clean heart over the old one by the top edge only. On it, write: *new heart; true heart in full assurance of faith; sprinkled clean from an evil conscience.*

**Ask** **Whose blood gives us access to God's holy places?** The blood of Jesus, the Lamb of God

**What did our great priest do for our sinful hearts?** Jesus sacrificed Himself to pay for our sins and to forgive them. In Baptism, our hearts are sprinkled clean with His blood and our bodies are washed with pure water. We receive His forgiveness and a true heart filled with sure faith.

Pull up the new heart to show the old, darkened heart.

**Say** **Our sinful hearts are filled with lust, anger, fear, idolatry, despair, evil conscience, jealousy, and more. God begins the removal process in the new heart He gives us in Christ. As we increase in spiritual health, many evils diminish, but they are not extinguished until we die. Spiritual health is nothing more than faith in or love in Christ** (AE 31:124, paraphrased)**.**

Cover the old heart again.

**Ask** **What does God extinguish in a clean heart?** An evil conscience. Mark out these words in the new heart.

**What is a true heart?** "An honest, believing heart" (*TLSB*, p. 2119; Hebrews 10:22 note). Circle "true heart" in the heart.

**Where do we get a true heart?** It is a gift of God by grace through faith in Christ, which we receive in God's Word and Sacraments (Ephesians 2:8–10).

**Say** **Although we sin, God does not forsake us. He made a way for us through Christ, His Son, and continues to care for us every day.**

# 4 Closing (3 minutes)

**Ask** **What did you learn about God's grace today?** Thank students who share.

To close, pray the Lord's Prayer or Apostles' Creed together.

## Faith in Action

Point out that as we leave Communion, where we have just received the forgiveness of our sins, the pastor says, "The body and blood of our Lord strengthen and preserve you steadfast in the true faith to life everlasting. Go in peace" (*LSB*, p. 164). Here, we see God once again preserving His people despite our sinfulness.

*Goes to the Heart*

# Lesson 4
# Cain and Abel

**Genesis 4:1–16**

## Heart-to-heart

**Mark 7:21–22:** [Jesus said,] "For from within, out of the heart of man, come evil thoughts, sexual immorality, theft, murder, adultery, coveting, wickedness, deceit, sensuality, envy, slander, pride, foolishness."

## Brother versus brother

### Read Genesis 4:1–2.

- Draw a large cookie-cutter-type outline of a person. Add details from these verses for your assigned brother, Cain or Abel.

- *Cain* sounds similar to the Hebrew phrase "I have gotten." Some scholars, including Martin Luther, think Eve believed she birthed the promised offspring who would defeat the devil and regain paradise (Genesis 3:15). If so, how do you think Adam and Eve treated Cain? Show this on your drawing of Cain.

- In Hebrew, *Abel* means "breath or vapor," implying something temporary. Show this on your drawing of Abel.

### Read Genesis 4:3–7.

- The Hebrew word translated as *had regard* means "looked at" or "paid attention to." Genesis does not say why God accepted Abel's sacrifice but not Cain's, so we let Scripture interpret Scripture.

  Read the following verses to find out why. Show these things on your drawings.

  **1 John 3:12:** We should not be like Cain, who was of the evil one and murdered his brother. And why did he murder him? Because his own deeds were evil and his brother's righteous.

  **Hosea 6:6:** [God said], "For I desire steadfast love and not sacrifice, the knowledge of God rather than burnt offerings."

  **1 Samuel 16:7:** For the LORD sees not as man sees: man looks on the outward appearance, but the LORD looks on the heart.

  **James 4:6:** God opposes the proud, but gives grace to the humble.

- How did Cain react to God's displeasure? Show Cain's reactions and your ideas on your drawing.

- God spoke Law to show Cain his sin so he would repent and come back to God. What did God warn Cain about?

### Read Genesis 4:8–16.

- How did Cain act out his emotions?

- What kind of criminal charge could we bring against Cain today?

- God knew where Abel was when He asked Cain where his brother was. Why did He ask? What did Cain do?

- What consequences did God give Cain for this sin?

- How did Cain react? What does this show was in Cain's heart? Show this on your drawing of Cain.

- How did God show mercy to Cain? Show this on your drawing of Cain.

## A true heart, a pure heart

**John 14:6:** Jesus said to him, "I am the way, and the truth, and the life. No one comes to the Father except through Me."

**Hebrews 10:19–22:** Therefore, brothers, since we have confidence to enter the holy places by the blood of Jesus, by the new and living way that He opened for us through the curtain, that is, through His flesh, and since we have a great priest over the house of God, let us draw near with a true heart in full assurance of faith, with our hearts sprinkled clean from an evil conscience and our bodies washed with pure water.

**Hebrews 12:22, 24:** You have come . . . to Jesus, the mediator of a new covenant, and to the sprinkled blood that speaks a better word than the blood of Abel.

# Preparing the Lesson

## Noah and the Flood

Genesis 6:1–9:17

## Key Point

In the flood, God destroyed sinful people. God's Son, Jesus, destroyed sin, once and for all, through His death and resurrection to give life to sinful people.

## Law/Gospel

God used water in a flood to drown sinful mankind. **In Baptism, God uses water to drown my sins, granting me eternal life through His Son, Jesus.**

## Context

As the tree is in the seed, so salvation history is in Genesis 1–11, including a universal judgment, a promise that a remnant shall be saved, and a new beginning.

## Commentary

In Genesis 6:1–4, the "sons of God" are probably the tribe of Adam who intermarry with "daughters of man" from the tribe of Cain. When people of faith marry unbelievers, their children get the impression that faith is something optional. Genesis 6:1–6 suggests that what is important among the generations before the flood are physical attraction, "renown," deeds of strength, and the glory of the flesh.

Noah, the last of Adam's line, "found favor" and "walked with God" (6:8–9). These expressions indicate that Noah's relationship with God is one of faith. By faith, he builds the ark that God uses to save him. Noah's family apparently share his faith in God and share in the work of building and filling the ark. They are saved as part of a faith community. Noah is not a sinless man, as shown in Genesis 9:18–29.

The word ark is best understood as box or container. The same word is used for Moses' basket. There are two of most animals aboard the ark, but seven pairs of clean (fit to eat) animals. God plans ahead for the time after the flood.

The text shows the flood beginning and then the animals with Noah's family entering the ark. God shuts them in (7:16). The forty days of floodwaters are echoed in forty years of Israel's wandering in the wilderness, forty days of fasting by our Lord, and our forty-day Lenten season.

Floodwaters come from above as rain and from below as springs. The destruction comes not gradually but in a violent rush. The earth, including hills and mountains, is covered with water. All breathing things on "dry land" (7:22) die because of man's sin.

Genesis 8:1 is a good example of how the Bible often speaks of God in human terms: "God remembered Noah." It may have appeared that God had forgotten about Noah until God acted on the ark's behalf. Note that the ark settles in the mountains of Ararat, a region around present-day Armenia.

The raven Noah sends out fails to return because it can live off of rotting flesh; the dove returns when it finds no suitable resting place. The second time, the dove returns with an olive leaf, a sign that God is at peace with the earth and that plants useful to humans are growing once again. The third time, the dove does not need to return.

Genesis 8:17 repeats the command to be fruitful and multiply. Noah offers a sacrifice of clean animals, which God finds pleasing because of Noah's faith (Hebrews 11:7), and God resolves not to punish the earth in this way for man's sake again, observing that "man's heart is evil from his youth" (Genesis 8:21).

Some traditions believe that the rainbow existed before the flood and was given new meaning; others regard it as being created at this time. What is clear is that the rainbow is now a sign of God's peace to the world and a promise that He will not again send a worldwide flood. It is a covenant to which God binds Himself and is not dependent on human works.

The elements present in the flood—water, renewal, death because of sin, salvation because of being joined to the people of faith, and God's unconditional promise of grace—are present in the Sacrament of Baptism (1 Peter 3:18–21).

**To hear an in-depth discussion of this Bible account, visit cph.org/podcast and listen to our Seeds of Faith podcast each week.**

Lesson 5

# Noah and the Flood

Genesis 6:1–9:17

## Get Ready
### Before Class

- Copy Student Page 5 for each person.

- For **Opening**, hang up several sheets of newsprint (masking tape) and get markers.

- For **God Speaks**, get Bibles, the Timeline Poster, newsprint, markers, and masking tape.

- For **We Live**, preview the YouTube video in the Old Testament 1 High School playlist at **bit.ly/1knXwnU**. To use it, get equipment ready (e.g., computer, tablet, Internet connection) and cue the video.

## **1** Opening (10 minutes)

### Too Much of a Good Thing

Gather near the newsprint sheet when ready to start.

**Say**  Pretend that we just found out we're going to receive a donation of fifty thousand gallons of milk with an expiration date in one week. Let's brainstorm ideas for how to use the milk before it expires. Remember, when brainstorming, we don't judge ideas. We write down everything.

Ask someone to be a timekeeper and to stop brainstorming at one minute. Write down every idea, no matter how ridiculous.

**Say**  Pick your favorite idea, and put a check mark by it on our list.

**Why did you pick this idea?** Let students share reasons.

**Are there any ideas that might be harmful?** Answers vary.

**In our sinful world, things created to bless us can actually cause harm, such as fifty thousand gallons of milk. Water is another. How does water bless us?** Our bodies are 65 percent water, and we need it every day. Water makes vegetation grow that provides shade, beauty, and food. It provides food and recreation. It keeps us cool on hot days and is necessary for life. We must have water, or we will die.

**How can water harm us?** Too much water causes plants to die. Floods and hurricanes destroy homes and communities, endanger life, and impede transportation. Water can cause death through drowning and disease.

**Say**  In today's lesson, we see how God used water to destroy and to save.

**Pray**  Dear God, help us to understand and believe that we can never get enough of the gifts You give us through Your Son and our Savior, Jesus. In His name we pray. Amen.

## **2** God Speaks (32 minutes)

### Downhill from Here

**Say**  After Cain killed Abel, Adam and Eve had a son named Seth, who carried forward the promise of the Savior and taught his children to worship God. The Bible calls Seth's descendants "sons of God." Cain's children, called "children of men," lived for themselves with little thought of God.

Hand out Bibles. Turn to **Genesis 6**. Ask volunteers to read **Genesis 6:1–2**.

**Ask**  **How did Seth's faithful children ("sons of God") begin to choose wives?** They chose "daughters of man" based on physical appearance.

**What did they not consider?** Whether the wives believed in God

**What did the sons of God gain and lose by marrying the unbelieving daughters of man?** They gained beautiful wives, but these unbelievers lived decadently, without regard for God. In time, Seth's children gave up faith-based living and did not teach their children to love God. Eventually, they fell away too. This reminds Christians to marry those who share our faith (2 Corinthians 6:14).

Be sensitive to students who may have one or both parents who do not believe in Jesus. Encourage them to love and obey their parents in Jesus' name. Paul said Christians married to unbelievers should live in peace and let their actions show God's love to their spouse (1 Corinthians 7:12–16).

**Say**  **God's Spirit would not abide in man forever. He gave humans 120 years to repent and return to Him. If not, they would completely reject Him.**

Ask a volunteer to read **Genesis 6:4**.

**Nephilim** were violent tyrants (*TLSB*, p. 24; 6:4 note). **What does "men of renown" mean?** People respected, revered, and admired these celebrities.

**We admire these kinds of people in our world too. Name some.** Answers might include mixed martial arts fighters; athletes; musicians; actors; criminals; and crooked business people and politicians. All may have impressive amounts of money or influence they flaunt without shame or regard for others.

Ask volunteers to read **Genesis 6:5–10** aloud.

**Ask**  **What grieved God?** Human wickedness, evil hearts, violence, and corruption of God-believers, which affected humanity and all creation.

**What did God decide to do?** Sorry for making humans, God decided to blot out (destroy) most humans, animals, birds, and creeping things.

**After 120 years, what one family remained faithful to the Lord?** Noah's

**Find four descriptions of Noah's faith.** (1) "Found favor in eyes of the LORD," (2) "a righteous man," (3) "blameless in his generation," and (4) "walked with God."

**What does it mean to be righteous?** *Righteous* describes "a person in a right relationship with God, trusting God's promised salvation and living by the covenant promise" (*TLSB*, p. 843; definition of *righteous*).

**Say**  **We often see cute Noah's ark pictures, toys, and wallpaper for children. But God's promised destruction through the flood wasn't winsome. It destroyed all living things except for the few kept alive in the ark.**

## High-Water Showdown

Show the Timeline Poster to demonstrate the lesson context.

Hand out Lesson 5 Student Page copies. Divide students into groups of two to five people. Assign each group a section on the Student Page

If you have fewer students, assign parts to individuals; or take one yourself.

Read the Student Page directions: **Read the Scripture passages, discuss the questions, and follow the directions.**

Point out the newsprint and markers. Give groups twenty minutes to work. As students work, help as needed and review questions to prepare for discussion.

## Key Point

In the flood, God destroyed sinful people. Jesus, His Son, destroyed sin, once and for all, in His death and resurrection, giving life to sinful people.

## Pronunciations

Ham: hamm
Japheth: JAY fehth
Nephilim: NEFF fill im
Shem: shim

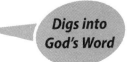

*Digs into God's Word*

## SECTION 1: Preparation, Genesis 6:13–7:16

▨ **What did God intend to do?** To destroy all flesh with the earth

▨ **Write a to-do list, showing what God told Noah to do.** Build an ark of gopher wood with three decks, rooms, and a roof, 300 × 50 × 30 cubits (450 × 75 × 45 feet). Cover it with pitch. Get two of every animal, bird, and creeping things, male and female. Store food.

▨ **What did God promise Noah (6:18)?** To establish a covenant with him; to save his family

▨ **How were animals collected (6:20)?** They came to Noah.

▨ **Why did God save Noah (7:1)?** Noah was righteous, justified by God's grace through faith.

▨ **Add the list of who and what went into the ark to the to-do list. (Clean animals were used for sacrifices.)** Seven pairs of clean animals, one pair of unclean animals, seven pairs of birds, Noah and his wife, Noah's sons and wives; 7:14 adds detail saying livestock, creeping things, and birds

▨ **How old was Noah when the flood started (7:11)? Add the date at the top of the list of ark riders.** Noah was six hundred years old. It started the seventeenth day of the second month.

▨ **Where did all the water come from?** Fountains of the great deep and windows of heaven opened, raining day and night. Luther said this was no ordinary rain; it was "a rain of the Lord's wrath" (AE 2:89).

▨ **Who shut the ark door (7:16)?** God

## SECTION TWO: Implementation, Genesis 7:17–8:19

▨ **Draw a timeline. Start with the day Noah went into the ark, in his six hundredth year, the second month, and the seventeenth day (7:11).**

▨ **On your timeline, show how long the rain fell (7:17).** Forty days

▨ **Mark the time (7:24) and water height (7:20) on your timeline. A cubit is about eighteen inches.** 150 more days; over twenty-two feet above the mountaintops

▨ **How did the floodwater both save and condemn?** The water God sent condemned the wicked but saved the righteous. The water lifted up Noah and his family while it drowned those who turned from God. In the flood, God destroyed sinful people.

▨ **What did God do to dry the earth (8:1–3)?** He sent a wind, closed the fountains of the deep, and stopped the rain.

▨ **Where did the ark land? Mark the date and the event on your timeline.** The ark landed on Mount Ararat on the seventeenth day of the seventh month.

▨ **On your timeline, mark the date the mountaintops appeared (8:5).** The first day of the tenth month

▨ **Forty days later, Noah sent out the raven (8:6–7). Mark this on your timeline. The scavenging raven found lots to eat and stayed near the ark until the land dried, but did not come back.**

▨ **Noah sent a dove out too, but she came back. Add the dove's second and third trips to the timeline with their outcomes.** Seven days later, the dove came back with a fresh olive leaf, showing that plants were returning. The third time, a week later, the dove didn't return, showing that the waters had receded.

**Growing in CHRIST.**

▨ **On your timeline, mark the day Noah saw dry ground (8:13).** Noah's 601st year, first month, first day, which was his birthday.

▨ **On your timeline, mark the day God told Noah to leave the ark (8:14–15).** Twenty-seventh day of the second month

**SECTION THREE: Aftermath, Genesis 8:20–9:17**

▨ **What did Noah do after he came out of the ark?** He built an altar to the Lord and sacrificed some clean animals and birds as burnt offerings.

▨ **What did God say about people and promise (8:21–22)?** The human heart is evil from youth. God would never again curse the ground because of humans. He would never again strike down every living creature. Seasons and days would remain as long as the earth does.

▨ **What did God say to bless Noah (vv. 1, 7)? Where have we heard this before?** Be fruitful and multiply. God commanded the same to Adam and Eve.

▨ **Make a menu that shows what God said the people could eat and not eat (9:2–4). How was this different from Adam and Eve's instructions (Genesis 1:30)?** God said to eat birds, animals, fish, ground creepers, and green plants. Previously, He told Adam and Eve to eat only plants as food.

▨ **Why did God say not to eat food with blood in it (9:4)?** Because life is in blood

▨ **Why did God say not to kill?** God made man in His own image. Those who shed the life of another should have their own blood shed.

▨ **What covenant did God make with man and all creatures? What sign did He give of this covenant?** God promised not to destroy the earth and all flesh again with water. He gave the rainbow as a sign of that promise.

## Debriefing

Call students back and post the newsprint sheets in Scripture order. Chronologically, let groups show their to-do lists, timelines, and menus and report on their section. As they do, ask questions about their section and correct misunderstandings.

When all have presented, thank them for their work. Then continue with this summarizing question, which is not on the Student Page.

**Ask**   **What do you think motivated Noah and kept him on task? Read Hebrews 11:7 (Student Page).** Students may suggest motivations such as the desire to stay alive, but in the final analysis, Noah received God's grace by faith and believed God's words and promises. These kept him focused. It must have been hard when surrounded by such temptations and wickedness.

*Goes to the Heart*

 **3 We Live** (15 minutes)

## Living like Noah

Questions are not on the Student Page, but Scripture verses are.

**Say**   **We have a lot in common with Noah. We live in a world filled with violence and sin; yet we have hope in Christ, our Savior.**

If you do not use the video, continue by reading **Psalm 40:2** (Student Page).

### Key Point

In the flood, God destroyed sinful people. Jesus, His Son, destroyed sin, once and for all, in His death and resurrection, giving life to sinful people.

*Goes to the Heart*

### Faith in Action

If time permits, go into your sanctuary to look at your baptismal font and see if it has eight sides to remind us of the eight people God saved from the flood. If time is short, ask students to look at the font on their own. Ask them to listen carefully to the liturgy in the next Baptism they witness to hear again why we receive Baptism and the promises and gifts God offers in it.

Show the Lesson 5 YouTube video, "Rescued" (2:34), in the Old Testament 1 High School playlist at **bit.ly/1knXwnU**. It shows the results of sin in the world and shows **Psalm 40:2** over an image of Christ crucified. Point out **Psalm 40:2** on Student Page.

**Ask** **How has God brought you out of the pit of destruction, the miry bog, and set your feet upon a rock?** Answers vary. Encourage students to talk about specific times in their lives, as well as how Jesus' death on the cross rescued us from the miry bog of sin and the pit of death.

**Like Noah, God gathers us into an ark, a safe place called His Church. How does God feed, protect, and save us there?** Through His Church on earth (an ark), God provides the means of salvation and gives us gifts that strengthen our faith. In Baptism, God gives eternal life, forgives sin, and makes us His family.

The preaching of God's Word strengthens our faith, and in Holy Communion, our sins are forgiven. God uses these gifts, as well as the Christian community at church, to strengthen us and provide for us while we live on earth.

God promises to never leave us or forsake us. His Word tells us He loves us, and He proved it by sending His Son, Jesus, to pay for our sins and offer forgiveness of sin to all believers. His Word comforts, assures, encourages, equips, and motivates us to serve and live as His people.

Read together **1 Peter 3:20–21** (Student Page).

**Ask** **God saved Noah with water. How did God save us by water?** In Baptism, God saves us. The old Adam drowns, and the new man rises to life in Christ. The same water that kills sin saves God's people, just as the same flood that killed many saved Noah and his family (God's people).

**What gifts do we receive at Baptism?** Baptism works forgiveness of sins, rescues from death and the devil, and gives eternal salvation. The Holy Spirit also begins working within us and gives us many other spiritual gifts, now and as we grow in knowledge and grace in the Lord Jesus Christ.

**How are you daily re-created in your Baptism?** The old Adam (sinful nature) is drowned by daily contrition (sorrow and confession of sins) and repentance. The new man is raised to life as God forgives our sins and as we grow in faith. Christ buried our sin with His death and gives us new life in His resurrection.

**Say** **Many baptismal fonts have eight sides. These eight sides symbolize two things. First, they remind us of the eight faithful survivors of the flood.**

**Second, they symbolize the eighth day of creation, when God began again with Noah and his family. The flood enabled the world to begin again, and so does Baptism. It raises us as new life. Before, we were dead to sin; now, we are alive in Christ.**

## 4 Closing (3 minutes)

**Ask** **What did you learn about Noah and the flood that you didn't know before?** Thank students who share.

**Pray** **Dear God, thank You for sending Your Son, Jesus, to destroy sin and death once and for all and for saving us in the waters of our Baptism. May we remain in Your grace always. In Jesus' name we pray. Amen.**

# Lesson 5
# Noah and the flood

Genesis 6:1–9:17

## High-water showdown

**Directions:** Read the Scripture passages, discuss the questions, and follow the directions.

### SECTION ONE: Preparation, Genesis 6:13–7:16

▧ What did God intend to do?

▧ Write a to-do list, showing what God told Noah to do.

▧ What did God promise Noah (6:18)?

▧ How were animals collected (6:20)?

▧ Why did God save Noah (7:1)?

▧ Add the list of who and what went into the ark to the to-do list. (Clean animals were used for sacrifices.)

▧ How old was Noah when the flood started (7:11)? Add the date at the top of the list of ark riders.

▧ Where did all the water come from?

▧ Who shut the ark door (7:16)?

### SECTION TWO: Implementation, Genesis 7:17–8:19

▧ Draw a timeline. Start with the day Noah went into the ark, in his six hundredth year, the second month, and the seventeenth day (7:11).

▧ On your timeline, show how long the rain fell (7:17).

▧ Mark the time (7:24) and water height (7:20) on your timeline. A cubit is about eighteen inches.

▧ How did the floodwater both save and condemn?

▧ What did God do to dry the earth (8:1–3)?

▧ Where did the ark land? Mark the date and event on your timeline.

▧ On your timeline, mark the date the mountaintops appeared (8:5).

▧ Forty days later, Noah sent out the raven (8:6–7). Mark this on your timeline. The scavenging raven found lots to eat and stayed near the ark until the land dried, but did not come back

▧ Noah sent a dove out too, but she came back. Add the dove's second and third trips to the timeline with their outcomes.

▧ On your timeline, mark the day Noah saw dry ground (8:13).

▧ On your timeline, mark the day God told Noah to leave the ark (8:14).

### SECTION THREE: Aftermath, Genesis 8:20–9:17

▧ What did Noah do after he came out of the ark?

▧ What did God say about people and promise (8:21–22)?

▧ What did God say to bless Noah (9:1, 7)? Where have we heard this before?

▧ Make a menu that shows what God said the people could eat and not eat (9:2–4)? How was this different from Adam and Eve's instructions (Genesis 1:30)?

▧ Why did God say not to eat food with blood in it (9:4)?

▧ Why did God say not to kill?

▧ What covenant did God make with man and all creatures? What sign did He give of this covenant?

### Debriefing

**Hebrews 11:7:** By faith Noah, being warned by God concerning events as yet unseen, in reverent fear constructed an ark for the saving of his household. By this he condemned the world and became an heir of the righteousness that comes by faith.

## Living like Noah

**Psalm 40:2:** He drew me up from the pit of destruction, out of the miry bog, and set my feet upon a rock, making my steps secure.

**1 Peter 3:20–21:** God's patience waited in the days of Noah, while the ark was being prepared, in which a few, that is, eight persons, were brought safely through water.

Baptism, which corresponds to this, now saves you, not as a removal of dirt from the body but as an appeal to God for a good conscience, through the resurrection of Jesus Christ.

# Preparing the Lesson

## God's Covenant with Abram

Genesis 12:1–9; 15:1–6; 17

## Key Point

God chose Abram (Abraham) and gave him faith to trust His promises to save His people. God gives us faith in Jesus, our Savior.

## Law/Gospel

In my sin, I doubt that God can do what He promises and do not trust Him. **God in His mercy carries out His promises and gives me faith in and through Jesus to trust Him.**

## Context

Genesis 1–11 describes the creation of the world and the history of all humanity. Genesis 12 begins a new era. God calls one person, Abram, to be the physical and spiritual father of His chosen people. God will work through Abram and his descendants to bring salvation for all. Abram's line culminates in Jesus Christ (Matthew 1:1–2; Romans 9:5), the offspring promised to Eve. True God and true man, Jesus brings forgiveness of sins and eternal life to all believers. All who are baptized into Christ are Abram's spiritual offspring and heirs of God's promises to Abram (Galatians 3:26–29).

## Commentary

In Genesis 12, God calls Abram to leave his homeland and go to a new land. Abram must travel and live by faith, since he does not know where God will lead him. God promises to bless others through Abram and his offspring.

In Genesis 15, the word of the Lord comes to Abram in a vision, assuring him there is nothing to fear. But Abram does fear because he has no son. God tells Abram to number the stars and promises that his offspring will be as numerous as those stars. "And [Abram] believed the Lord, and He counted it to him as righteousness" (Genesis 15:6). Paul quotes this verse in Romans 4:3 and Galatians 3:6 to show that Abram was justified—that is, declared righteous before God—not by works, but by faith in God's promises, including the promise of the Savior, who was to come from Abram's own descendants.

The Lord assures Abram that He will give him the land of Canaan. Abram asks how he can be certain. God pledges His faithfulness by means of a covenant in which God confirms His promises with a solemn ceremony that includes sacrifice. The Lord tells Abram that after his descendants have sojourned in another land for four hundred years, God will give them Canaan as their possession.

As time elapses, Sarai remains childless, so she gives her maidservant Hagar to Abram so that Hagar might bear him a son. Ishmael is born when Abram is eighty-six. When Abram is ninety-nine years old, God changes his name from Abram ("exalted father") to Abraham ("father of a multitude"). God seals His covenant with Abraham by telling him that he and all of his male descendants are to be circumcised as "a sign of the covenant between Me and you" (17:11).

God also changes Sarai's name to Sarah (both mean "princess") and promises that kings shall come from her. Abraham laughs, perhaps in joyful confidence that the Lord will perform this miracle or perhaps with a degree of skepticism. Abraham then asks for God's blessing on Ishmael.

God confirms that He will indeed bless Ishmael but that He will establish His everlasting covenant with a son born to Sarah (to be named Isaac). Through Isaac, God would fulfill His greatest promise: that from Abraham and Sarah's descendants would be born the Savior, Jesus, in whom all the nations of the earth would be blessed through the forgiveness of sins.

**To hear an in-depth discussion of this Bible account, visit cph.org/podcast and listen to our Seeds of Faith podcast each week.**

# God's Covenant with Abram

Genesis 12:1–9; 15:1–6; 17

## Get Ready

**Before Class**

- Copy Student Page 6 for each person.

- For **Opening**, bring a piece of candy or gum in a flavor you know most people don't like, such as black licorice or hot cinnamon.

- For **God Speaks**, get Bibles, the Timeline Poster, newsprint, masking tape, and markers.

  At the top of a piece of newsprint, write *God's promises to Abram*. Write the numbers *1–7* down the side. Hang it up.

- For **We Live**, preview the YouTube video in the Old Testament 1 High School playlist at **bit.ly/1knXwnU**. To use it, get equipment ready (e.g., computer, tablet, Internet connection) and cue the video.

##  1 Opening (10 minutes)

### Gifts and Choices

Use this activity to show that we're all sinners who need grace. God offers His gifts in Christ to all people, but some reject Him.

**Say**  I have a treat for you this morning. Walk around the room and personally offer the spicy gum or candy to everyone. Do a "hard sell."

**Why did some of you refuse the treat?** Let students share.

**You really had only one choice with my treat: to reject it. I gave it to you. It's yours any time you want it. You didn't have to earn it.**

**This reminds me of people who refuse or reject God's gift of salvation in Christ. God wants all people to be saved and know His truth** (1 Timothy 2:3–4). **He offers everyone the same gift, yet some reject Him. What reasons have you heard people give for not believing?** Encourage sharing.

**Why do you think God doesn't just *make* everyone believe in Him?** Encourage sharing. God doesn't want people to love Him because they have to.

**So why do you think some people believe in God while others reject Him?** The Holy Spirit works through God's Word and Sacraments to make Christians when and where He pleases. God's Word sounds foolish to unbelievers (1 Corinthians 2:4). Over time, hearts may become hardened to God's grace.

**You can't tell if a person believes by just looking at the person. People can live an outwardly decent life, but only the Holy Spirit gives new life and a new heart** (John 3:5).

**Pray**  God our Father, open our hearts to hear and believe Your Word, to trust You in all things, and to know that You are the giver of all good gifts. In Jesus' name we pray. Amen.

##  2 God Speaks (35 minutes)

### Great God, Great Promises

Stand by the newsprint sheet you prepared, as directed in Get Ready.

**Say**  Today, we meet Abram, a idolater God called to follow Him (Joshua 24:2).

Show the Timeline Poster, and note the approximate dates.

Hand out Bibles. Ask students to turn to **Genesis 12** and read aloud **verses 1–7**. Recruit a scribe to write on the newsprint, if you like.

**Growing in CHRIST.**

**Say** **Let's find seven promises the Lord made to Abram.** As students find the promises, write them on the newsprint.

1. I will show you the land, where to go (v. 1).
2. I will make you a great nation (v. 2).
3. I will bless you and make your name great (v. 2).
4. I will bless those who bless you (v. 3).
5. I will curse those who dishonor you (v. 3).
6. In you, all families of the earth will be blessed (v. 3).
7. To your offspring I will give this land (v. 7).

**The name of God used here, "Lord," written in small caps or all caps, indicates the Hebrew word *Yahweh*, which is the personal name of God. What does this tell us?** God personally, intimately connected with Abram.

**Abram was a childless seventy-five-year-old when God called and led him to Canaan. Ten years after God promised to make Abram a great nation, Abram still had no children and God made a formal covenant with him.**

Hand out Student Page 6 copies, which include the covenant description, but not the questions for **Genesis 15**.

Ask a volunteer to read the covenant description from the Student Page. Then recruit volunteers to read **Genesis 15:1–6** as narrator, God, and Abram.

**Ask** **Whom was the covenant between?** Abram and the Lord

**What was Abram's concern?** He had no child or heir except Eliezer, his servant.

**What promises did the Lord give Abram?** God would shield him and give him a great reward (v. 1). Eliezer would not be his heir; God would give him a son. God showed him the stars, and promised to give him as many offspring as them.

**Later in the chapter, God promised to give the land of Canaan to Abram's offspring, and Abraham offered a sacrifice that the Lord accepted. It confirmed the covenant. How did Abram respond to God's promises?** He believed the Lord, who counted it to him as righteousness.

**What is righteousness?** Write *righteousness* on the newsprint. Share ideas.

**Say** ***Righteousness* means "proved right" or "in good order." It describes a right relationship with God that trusts His salvation and promises** (*TLSB*, p. 843; definition of *righteous*).

**God counts those who believe in Jesus as righteous. This is God's free gift to us by grace through faith in Christ, who died for our sins and rose from the dead. Abram looked forward to the promised Savior, Jesus. We look back and believe in Jesus, our Savior and Lord.**

**Righteousness is not based on our behavior or actions, as Abram and Sarai showed when they tried to help God keep His promise of a son. Sarai gave Abram her Egyptian servant Hagar as a concubine; Hagar gave birth to a son, Ishmael, when Abram was eighty-six years old. Was this right or wrong?** Affirm that it was against God's moral law to take more than one wife. Their actions also showed a lack of trust in God to keep His promises.

**God graciously reserved punishment for their sins and kept His promise. He does the same for us as we struggle to trust Him.**

Divide students into groups of two to five people, or continue as a large group.

*Digs into God's Word*

## Key Point

God chose Abram (later called Abraham) and gave him faith to trust His promises to save His people. God gives us faith in Jesus, our Savior.

## Pronunciations

Abram: A bruhm
Ai: A eye
Bethel: BETH uhl
Canaan: KANE un
Canaanites:
    KANE un ites
Damascus:
    duh MASS cuss
Eliezer: el ih EE zur
Haran: HAIR uhn
Isaac: EYE zik
Ishmael: IHSH may ell
Moreh: MORE ay
Negeb: NEG eb
Sarai: SARE eye
Shechem: SHEK uhm

## Key Point

God chose Abram (later called Abraham) and gave him faith to trust His promises to save His people. God gives us faith in Jesus, our Savior.

*Digs into God's Word*

Read together the covenant parts at the top of the Student Page 6. Then read the Student Page directions: **Read Genesis 17 verses and discuss questions. List the number of the covenant part(s) after each question.**

Tell groups they have twenty minutes to work. As students work, help as needed, and review the questions to prepare for discussion.

**1–4**  **Thirteen more years passed after Ishmael's birth, but God still did not give Abram and Sarai a son. Now the Lord came to establish a covenant. Whom was it between?** The Lord and Abraham (covenant part 1)

**In this covenant, what did God ask from Abram?** For Abram to walk before Him and be blameless (covenant part 2)

**What did God promise to do for Abram?** Multiply him greatly (covenant part 2)

**What did Abram's action show?** Falling on his face showed respect, fear, humility, and awe in the presence of God (covenant part 3).

**5–8**  **Abram means "exalted father." Abraham means "father of many." How was changing Abram's name a sign of God's promises?** God would make Abram the father of a multitude of nations (covenant parts 2 and 3).

**What other promises did God make?** God promised to make Abraham fruitful; nations and kings would come from him; the covenant would transfer to Abraham's offspring for everlasting; He would be God of Abram and his offspring; the land of Canaan would become an everlasting possession (covenant part 2).

**Who else was included in the covenant?** Abraham's offspring (covenant part 1)

**9–14**  **What did God tell Abraham and his offspring to do as a sign to remember the covenant?** Circumcise every male, eight days or older. Speak honestly with teens about circumcision, the surgical removal of the foreskin, a common practice in the world even today (covenant 3).

**What kinds of rituals or reminders do we use to remember and keep promises?** We might pinky swear or cross our heart to confirm promises. An engagement ring seals a promise. Some people wear jewelry or get tattoos to remind them of a person, a promise, a Bible verse, or something they value. Seeing the item reminds them of this every day (covenant part 3).

**15–27**  **God told Abraham to change Sarai's name to Sarah, which means "princess." How was this new name a sign of God's promises to her?** God would bless Sarah; He would give her a child with Abraham; nations and kings would come from her lineage (covenant parts 2 and 3).

**How did Abraham react to the news that Sarah and he would yet have a baby? Why?** Abraham fell on his face again, but this time he laughed. He wondered how old people like them could have a baby.

**What alternative plan did Abraham offer?** Abraham asked God just to count Ishmael as the promised son.

**What promises did God offer in response?** God did not chastise Abraham for laughing or offering Ishmael, but He refused the offer. Sarah would have a baby and name him Isaac. God would establish an everlasting covenant with Isaac and his offspring. God promised to make Ishmael fruitful, multiply his family, and make him the father of twelve princes and a great nation (covenant part 2).

**When did the Lord say Sarah would bear Isaac?** This time, next year

**What did Abraham do to keep his part of the covenant right away?** He, Ishmael, and all the males in his household were circumcised.

**Growing in Christ**

## Debriefing

When time elapses, come back together, even if everyone didn't finish. Discuss the details of each part of the covenant: parties involved; oaths or promises; and signs or actions, as indicated in the answers above. You may need to help students see the name changes as signs and promises.

# 3 We Live (12 minutes)

## A New Covenant

**Say** Jesus fulfilled Abraham's covenant. He is the promised offspring, the King of kings who gives Abraham more descendants than the stars.

Jesus gave a new covenant in the Lord's Supper. He confirmed the covenant a few hours later with action in His sacrificial death and resurrection.

> **Goes to the Heart**

**Say** Let's identify the parts of this new covenant. Ask volunteers to read **Luke 22:19–20** and **1 Corinthians 11:23–26** (Student Page).

**Parties involved:** Jesus and His disciples (including us)

**Oaths or promises:** forgiveness of sins; remember

**Signs or actions that confirm the covenant:** We eat bread/His body, drink wine/His blood

If you do not use the video, continue with the next "Say" statement.

Show the Lesson 6 YouTube video, "New Covenant (Yeshua) Joshua Aaron" (3:01), in the Old Testament 1 High School playlist at **bit.ly/1knXwnU**.

**Ask** What does the video say about Jesus? Jesus (Yeshua, a Hebrew version of the name) offers a new covenant (1 Corinthians 11:25) that fulfills Old Testament prophets (Jeremiah 31:31–34; Isaiah 49:6).

**Say** Luther said the new covenant also includes Baptism. Ask a volunteer to read the Luther quote from the Student Page.

**Ask** How can our Baptism remind us every day that God made a new covenant with us in Christ Jesus that promises forgiveness of sins and eternal life? Tell students we can draw an invisible cross over our heart and on our forehead to remember we received "the sign of the holy cross both upon your forehead and upon your heart to mark you as one redeemed by Christ the crucified" (LSB, p. 268). When we confess our sins in church or personally each day, we remember that God forgives our sins for the sake of Christ and began this work in us at Baptism.

**Say** Sometimes, Abram doubted before he believed. As believers in Christ, that happens to us too. Sin severely impairs our hearing and believing. Even in those times, God's Word and promises are still ours through our Baptism. However great our sin, He delivers forgiveness, life, and salvation.

### Faith in Action

Show students how to make the sign of the cross. Using three fingers, touch the forehead and move the hand down to the chest. Then touch the left shoulder; then right shoulder. Tell them they can make this sign whenever they hear or speak the name of the triune God, to remember their Baptism—morning, evening (or anytime), and before prayers (including meal prayers).

# 4 Closing (3 minutes)

**Ask** What did you learn today about God's promises? Thank students who share.

To close, pray the Lord's Prayer together (Student Page).

# Lesson 6
# God's covenant with Abram Genesis 12:1–9; 15:1–6; 17

**A covenant** is a solemn agreement or contract that usually included

1. a list of the parties involved;
2. oaths or promises (what each would do);
3. signs or actions of confirmation.

## Great God, great promises

**Directions:** Read **Genesis 17** verses and discuss questions. List the number of the covenant part(s) after each question.

### Verses 1–4

▓ Thirteen more years passed after Ishmael's birth, but God still did not give Abram and Sarai a son. Now the Lord came to establish a covenant. Whom was it between?

▓ In this covenant, what did God ask from Abram?

▓ What did God promise to do for Abram?

### Verses 5–8

▓ What did Abram's action show (v. 3)?

▓ Abram means "exalted father," but Abraham means "father of many." How was changing Abram's name a sign of God's promises?

▓ What other promises did God make?

▓ Who else was included in the covenant?

### Verses 9–14

▓ What did God tell Abraham and his offspring to do as a sign to remember the covenant?

▓ What kinds of rituals or reminders do we use to remember and keep promises?

### Verses 15–27

▓ God told Abraham to change Sarai's name to Sarah, which means "princess." How was this new name a sign of God's promises to her?

▓ How did Abraham react to the news that Sarah and he would yet have a baby? Why?

▓ What alternative plan did Abraham offer?

▓ What promises did God offer in response?

▓ When did the Lord say Sarah would bear Isaac?

▓ What did Abraham do to keep his part of the covenant right away?

## A new covenant

▓ Identify parts of this new covenant.

▓ Parties involved

▓ Oaths or promises

▓ Signs or actions that confirm the covenant

**Luke 22:19–20:** And [Jesus] took bread, and when He had given thanks, He broke it and gave it to them, saying, "This is My body, which is given for you. Do this in remembrance of Me." And likewise the cup after they had eaten, saying, "This cup that is poured out for you is the new covenant in My blood."

**1 Corinthians 11:23–26:** The Lord Jesus on the night when He was betrayed took bread, and when He had given thanks, He broke it, and said, "This is My body which is for you. Do this in remembrance of Me." In the same way also He took the cup, after supper, saying, "This cup is the new covenant in My blood. Do this, as often as you drink it, in remembrance of me." For as often as you eat this bread and drink the cup, you proclaim the Lord's death until He comes.

▓ Luther said, "Abraham had circumcision as the sign of this promise. We have Baptism, which was instituted with a far more magnificent form; for we are baptized in the name of the Father, of the Son, and of the Holy Spirit" (AE 3:123–24).

▓ How can our Baptism remind us every day that God made a new covenant with us in Christ Jesus that promises forgiveness of sins and eternal life?

## The Lord's Prayer

Our Father who art in heaven, hallowed be Thy name, Thy kingdom come, Thy will be done on earth as it is in heaven; give us this day our daily bread; and forgive us our trespasses as we forgive those who trespass against us; and lead us not into temptation, but deliver us from evil. For Thine is the kingdom and the power and the glory forever and ever. Amen.

Growing in Christ® High School © 2014, 2016 Concordia Publishing House. Scripture: ESV®. Catechism quotation: © 1986 CPH. Luther's Works quotation: © 1968 CPH. Reproduced by permission.

# Preparing the Lesson

## Abraham's Visitors from Heaven

Genesis 18:1–15; 21:1–7

## Key Point

God came to Abraham with the promise of a son. Abraham's descendant, our Lord Jesus, comes to us in Word and Sacraments, telling us that in Him all things are possible.

## Law/Gospel

I sin by doubting God's Word and promises, thinking He cannot do what He says. **As God's child, I have nothing to fear because God is faithful and His Word is true. He has kept His promise to send His Son, Jesus, to be my Savior, and through Him, He gives me the joy of His salvation.**

## Context

In Genesis 17, God had promised Abraham: "Sarah your wife shall bear you a son, and you shall call his name Isaac. . . . I will establish My covenant with Isaac, whom Sarah shall bear to you at this time next year" (vv. 19, 21). Now, the Lord reaffirms that promise.

## Commentary

While Abraham is sitting by the door of his tent in the heat of the day, three visitors appear. One of them is identified in Genesis 18:1, 10, 13, and 14 as "the Lord" (Yahweh). The other two are angels (Genesis 19:1). Abraham shows his guests legendary Middle Eastern hospitality by arranging for a meal for them. The writer to the Hebrews encourages us to do likewise: "Do not neglect to show hospitality to strangers, for thereby some have entertained angels unawares" (13:2).

Abraham arranges a generous feast and stands humbly by, taking the role of a servant while his guests eat. The guests then ask the whereabouts of Sarah, who is listening from the tent. Sarah hears the Lord repeat His promise that He will return to Abraham about this time next year and that Sarah will give birth to a son. Since Sarah is well past her childbearing years, she laughs in disbelief.

The omniscient Lord, however, knows about her laughter and the underlying unbelief, and He addresses her through Abraham: "Why did Sarah laugh and say, 'Shall I indeed bear a child, now that I am old?'" (Genesis 18:13). The gracious Lord is not interested in exposing Sarah's unbelief for the sake of shaming her, but in order that she might recognize her sinful unbelief and turn from it to faith in God's promises and His power to accomplish them. He continues, "Is anything too hard for the Lord? At the appointed time I will return to you, about this time next year, and Sarah shall have a son" (18:14).

However, Sarah still tries to cover up her sin and denies laughing. The Lord again confronts her with His knowledge that she did laugh. The name God decreed for her son (17:19), Isaac, means "he laughs." It will be a lifelong reminder to her both of her sinful mistrust and of the Lord's mercy to her in spite of it. The writer to the Hebrews tells us that the Lord did kindle faith in Sarah: "By faith Sarah herself received power to conceive, even when she was past the age, since she considered Him faithful who had promised" (11:11).

Genesis 21 records the fulfillment of God's promise. The Lord visited Sarah in grace and enabled her to give birth to Isaac, the son through whom God would ultimately fulfill His greatest promise to Abraham. God would bless all the families of the earth (Genesis 12:3) with salvation by sending Jesus, "the son of Isaac, the son of Abraham" (Luke 3:34), "the son of God" (3:38).

**To hear an in-depth discussion of this Bible account, visit cph.org/podcast and listen to our Seeds of Faith podcast each week.**

# Abraham's Visitors from Heaven

Genesis 18:1–15; 21:1–7

## Get Ready
### Before Class

- Copy Student Page 7 for each person.

- For **Opening**, preview the YouTube video in the Old Testament 1 High School playlist at **bit.ly/1knXwnU**. To use it, get equipment ready (e.g., computer, tablet, Internet connection) and cue the video.

- For **God Speaks**, get Bibles, the Timeline Poster, newsprint, masking tape, and markers.

  Hang up a sheet of newsprint and write nine blanks for the letters of the word *theophany*.

- For **We Live**, continue to use Bibles, markers, and student tree pictures from God Speaks.

## ① Opening (10 minutes)

### What Are Angels?

Welcome students as they arrive. When ready, gather everyone together.

**Say** Our lesson today includes a visit by angels. **What are angels?** Let students share their ideas, and do not correct misconceptions yet.

**Often, when someone dies, we hear people say that person has become an angel. This happened when actor Paul Walker died in a tragic car crash. Let's see more in our video.**

Show the Lesson 7 YouTube video, "Paul Walker—Do People Become Angels?" (2:07), in the Old Testament 1 High School playlist at **bit.ly/1knXwnU**.

Ask if students have any questions. Discuss concerns.

**Say** The angels in our lesson today were never human, but surprisingly, they brought someone with them who became human one day.

**Pray** Lord God, give us discernment to tell Your truth from error, to know Your love and grace, to live as Your people. In Jesus' name we pray. Amen.

## ② God Speaks (35 minutes)

### Theophany

Stand by your newsprint sheet with the nine blanks for letters (*theophany*). Hand out Bibles and Student Page 7 copies.

**Say** Guess this word that describes encounters with God, many of which we've talked about this quarter. As you give clues, let students guess letters and fill in the blanks. We use this word to describe Adam and Eve talking to God; or Cain speaking to God after he killed his brother Abel; or God telling Noah to build an ark; or God speaking to Abram. Fill in all letters.

**Ask** What is a theophany? An appearance or encounter with God. *Theo* means "God" in Greek.

**Why do you think God doesn't appear or speak directly to us any longer?** Let students share their ideas.

Ask volunteers to read **Hebrews 1:1–3** (Student Page).

**What do these verses say about God speaking to us?** God has spoken to us by His Son. We learn about Jesus from the Bible, God's true Word.

**Ask** **What does Hebrews 1 say Jesus did for us?** Through Him, God created the world. He upholds the universe. He made purification for sins.

**Would you rather hear God's Word from His prophets, from Jesus, or from the Bible?** Let students share their opinions. Help students see that God's Word in the Bible contains all of these.

**Say** **In our lesson, we hear how Abraham met the preincarnate Christ and two angels. Jesus is the greatest theophany!** *Preincarnate* **means "before having human flesh"; in other words, before Jesus came to earth as a baby.**

## Three Visitors Deliver a Message

Show the Timeline Poster to demonstrate the lesson context.

Hand out Bibles. Divide into groups of two to five people.

If you prefer to stay in one group, read, discuss, and make one tree together.

Read Student Page directions: **Read Genesis 18 verses, discuss questions, and follow directions.** Students draw a large tree and add details; also used in We Live.

*Digs into God's Word*

Point out the newsprint and markers. Tell students they have twenty minutes to work. As students do, help as needed and prepare for discussion.

**1–8** **Abraham's family camped near the oak trees of Mamre. On a separate sheet of paper, draw a large tree.**

**When did Abraham first see the three men? Draw a sun that shows this time of day.** "The heat of the day," noon or early afternoon

**The rest of Genesis 18 and 19:1 show that two of the men were angels. Who was the third, according to 18:1?** The Lord

**Christ, before He was born in the flesh, sometimes appeared for short times and for specific reasons. Scripture identifies Him as the Lord here. (A theophany!) What did Abraham do to welcome the men and show hospitality?** He ran to them, bowed, and pleaded that they stop and visit. He said that if he found favor in their sight, then they shouldn't pass by their servant. He offered water to wash their feet, which a servant probably did. This was a common courtesy because the roads were dusty and people wore sandals. He also offered rest under the oak tree and a "morsel" of bread.

Abraham asked Sarah to make bread (cakes). He chose a calf and had a young man quickly prepare it. Abraham personally served the food to the men. This was well beyond the understated "morsel" Abraham offered. Abraham stood nearby, ready to do or get whatever they needed, like an on-call waiter. This showed great respect and hospitality.

**9–15** **It seems odd that the strangers knew Abraham's wife's name, but the Lord knows everything. What did He say about her?** The Lord said He would return about the same time next year and Sarah would have a son.

**What did Sarah do when she heard the Lord say she would have a baby?** Sarah laughed and spoke to herself.

**Who heard her laughter and words?** The Lord heard her laughter and words, just as He heard Abraham's hidden laughter and words in the lesson about God's covenant with Abram.

**Earlier, Abraham laughed when God promised a son. God said to name their baby Isaac, which means "laughter." What a perfect name for this**

### Key Point

God came to Abraham with the promise of a son. Abraham's descendant, our Lord Jesus, comes to us in Word and Sacraments, telling us that in Him all things are possible.

### Pronunciations

Mamre: MAM ray

## Key Point

God came to Abraham with the promise of a son. Abraham's descendant, our Lord Jesus, comes to us in Word and Sacraments, telling us that in Him all things are possible.

**Goes to the Heart**

**child! What did the Lord say in response to Sarah's laughter and words?** "Is anything too hard for the LORD?" In a year, Sarah would have a son.

**Add something to represent laughter on your drawing. Why did Sarah deny laughing?** She felt afraid.

**Just as God said, Isaac was born a year later. Write the parents' names on the tree base and Isaac's name on a main branch.**

**God hears our spoken, whispered, lip-synced, written, and texted words and thoughts. Does this comfort you or make you feel afraid, as it did Sarah? Add something to your drawing to show that God hears us.** Answers vary and will depend on whether individuals need to hear Law or Gospel at this point of the lesson.

**How did the Lord show hospitality to Sarah and Abraham?** Despite their sin, unbelief, and attempts to fix things, Abraham and Sarah were still loved by God. He told them they would soon have their son, Isaac, and He kept this promise. He also kept the promise to bring the Savior, Jesus, our Lord, from their lineage and to make them the ancestors of many kings and nations.

**How does God show us hospitality?** God shows this same grace in Christ Jesus by forgiving our sins and rescuing us from sin and death through Jesus' perfect life, sacrificial death, and victorious resurrection.

**Write Jesus' name coming off a branch from Isaac.**

**Add crosses on the tree to show that God accepts and welcomes us in Christ Jesus.**

## Debriefing

When time elapses, gather everyone together. Ask groups to hang up their trees. Give groups time to see other drawings. Discuss questions students may have. Especially discuss the last question about how God shows us hospitality.

## 3 We Live (12 minutes)

### Children of Abraham

Continue using Student Page 7. Questions are not on the page, but Scripture is.

**Ask** **How did Abraham's relationship with the Lord change over time?** As Abraham learned to rely on God, their relationship deepened. Abraham felt confident enough to tell the Lord what he really thought or needed. Their encounters became more like dialogues than God just giving directions.

**When God promised to give Abraham offspring, to whom did He refer? Read Galatians 3:16** (on Student Page)**.** Paul says the offspring is Jesus Christ, not Isaac. God said "through Isaac shall your offspring be named" (Genesis 21:12; Romans 9:7).

**New Testament religious leaders proudly proclaimed status as children of Abraham. Jesus disagreed, saying that if they were, they would listen to Him because He came from God** (John 8:34–59)**. So who are the children of Abraham? How did they become this? Read Galatians 3:13–14, 27–29** (Student Page)**.** Christ redeemed us so we might receive Abraham's blessing and

## Faith in Action

Encourage students to show hospitality to others as God shows hospitality to them. Help them list things they can do to show hospitality to guests at home (e.g., take their coats, ask them to sit down, offer a drink) and church (e.g., introduce themselves, talk to others, show visitors what to do and where to go). Help students focus on kindnesses that help others feel welcome and comfortable.

receive the promised Spirit through faith. The baptized in Christ are one in Him and, through Him, become children of Abraham.

**What special blessing connected to Abraham do we receive through Baptism?** Baptized and adopted into God's family, we are Abraham's children too and heirs of the promises God gave Him, especially to bless all the families of the world through Abraham's descendant and God's Son, Jesus.

Ask students to get their trees from God Speaks. Then ask students to write their own name and classmates' names on higher-up branches on the trees to show they are children of God and Abraham through faith in Jesus.

# 4 Closing (3 minutes)

**Say** **Name something that will stick with you from this lesson.** Thank students who share.

Close by reading **Galatians 3:27–29** aloud together (on Student Page). Pray the Lord's Prayer, if you like.

# Lesson 7
# Abraham's visitors from heaven
## Genesis 18:1–15; 21:1–7

## Theophany

**Hebrews 1:1–3:** Long ago, at many times and in many ways, God spoke to our fathers by the prophets, but in these last days He has spoken to us by His Son, whom He appointed the heir of all things, through whom also He created the world.

He is the radiance of the glory of God and the exact imprint of his nature, and He upholds the universe by the word of his power. After making purification for sins, He sat down at the right hand of the Majesty on high.

## Three visitors deliver a message

**Directions:** Read **Genesis 18** verses, discuss questions, and follow directions.

### Verses 1–8

- Abraham's family camped near the oak trees of Mamre. On a separate sheet of paper, draw a large tree.

- When did Abraham first see the three men? Draw a sun that shows this time of day.

- The rest of Genesis 18 and 19:1 show that two of the men were angels. Who was the third, according to 18:1?

- Christ, before He was born in flesh, sometimes appeared for a short time and a specific reason. Biblical scholars identify Him as the Lord here. (A theophany!) What did Abraham do to welcome the men and show hospitality?

### Verses 9–15

- It seems odd that the strangers knew Abraham's wife's name, but the Lord knows everything. What did He say about her?

- What did Sarah do when she heard the Lord say she would have a baby?

- Who heard her laughter and words?

- Earlier, Abraham laughed when God promised a son. God said to name their baby Isaac, which

means "laughter." What a perfect name for this child! What did the Lord say in response to Sarah's laughter and words?

- Add something to represent laughter on your drawing. Why did Sarah deny laughing?

- Just as God said, Isaac was born a year later. Write the parents' names on the tree base and Isaac's name on a main branch.

- God hears our spoken, whispered, lip-synced, written, and texted words and thoughts. Does this comfort you or make you feel afraid, as it did Sarah? Add something to your drawing to show that God hears us.

- How did the Lord show hospitality to Sarah and Abraham?

- How does God show us hospitality?

- Write Jesus' name coming off a branch from Isaac.

- Add crosses on the tree to show that God accepts and welcomes us in Christ Jesus.

## Children of Abraham

**Galatians 3:16:** Now the promises were made to Abraham and to his offspring. It does not say, "And to offsprings," referring to many, but referring to one, "And to your offspring," who is Christ.

**Galatians 3:13–14:** Christ redeemed us from the curse of the law by becoming a curse for us . . . so that in Christ Jesus the blessing of Abraham might come to the Gentiles, so that we might receive the promised Spirit through faith.

**Galatians 3:27–29:** For as many of you as were baptized into Christ have put on Christ. There is neither Jew nor Greek, there is neither slave nor free, there is no male and female, for you are all one in Christ Jesus. And if you are Christ's, then you are Abraham's offspring, heirs according to promise.

# Preparing the Lesson

## Abraham and Isaac

Genesis 21:1–7; 22:1–19

## Key Point

God provided a ram as a sacrifice for Abraham and Isaac. He provides the perfect sacrifice for our sin: His Son, Jesus, the Lamb of God.

## Law/Gospel

God requires a payment for my sin. **God sent His own Son, Jesus, to be sacrificed in payment for my sin.**

## Context

God's wonderful promises to Abraham in Genesis 12, including that He would make Abraham into a great nation (v. 2) and that in him all the families of the earth would be blessed (v. 3), hinge on Abraham having a son. Moreover, God said that this son would be borne by Abraham's wife, Sarah (17:19). Twenty-five years after God first made His promises, Abraham and Sarah (who is well past childbearing years) still have no son.

## Commentary

The Lord visits Sarah; that is, He draws near to her in grace and miraculously enlivens her dead womb, enabling her to conceive and bear a son. Abraham obeys God's commands regarding the child by naming him Isaac (in fulfillment of Genesis 17:19) and by circumcising him when he is eight days old (in fulfillment of 17:10–13). Isaac's name, which means "he laughs," evokes the laughter of joy at the birth of the miraculous child. Luther says this about the basis of Abraham's joy: "What thus far has been an object of hope, and what he has believed, this is now a reality; ... the promise has now been made flesh" (Luther's Works 4:4).

Abraham dearly loves his child of the promise. Does he, perhaps, love him more than he loves God? God tests Abraham's love by commanding him to offer Isaac as a burnt offering. Abraham immediately prepares to carry out God's command. But then how will God fulfill His promise that through Isaac Abraham would have many descendants

(Genesis 21:12)? God enables Abraham to trust that He will indeed fulfill His promise even if Isaac is sacrificed: Abraham "considered that God was able even to raise [Isaac] from the dead" (Hebrews 11:19).

Abraham and Isaac arrive at the place of sacrifice. It is called Moriah, the place where Abraham's descendant King David will one day build an altar at God's command (1 Chronicles 21:18–28). It is also the site where the city of Jerusalem will one day be founded and where Solomon's temple will be built (2 Chronicles 3:1).

At Moriah, Abraham prepares the altar, binds his son in the manner of an animal sacrifice, and raises the knife to slay him. But the Angel of the Lord (actually a manifestation of God Himself) calls to Abraham from heaven, telling him not to lay a hand on the boy: "For now I know that you fear God, seeing you have not withheld your son, your only son, from Me" (Genesis 22:12).

Abraham lifts his eyes and sees a ram. As Abraham had earlier assured Isaac (22:8), God provided the sacrifice, and Abraham offers it up in place of his son. Again, the Lord calls to Abraham, confirming His earlier promises. Through Abraham's offspring, all the nations of the earth would be blessed. God fulfilled that promise by sending the Savior of the world of sinners, Jesus, from the line of Abraham (Matthew 1:1).

As Abraham laid the wood of the burnt offering on his only son, whom he loved, so God willingly laid the wood of the cross on His only Son, whom He loved. But unlike Isaac, for whom God provided a substitute, Jesus was sacrificed. He is "the Lamb of God, who takes away the sin of the world!" (John 1:29).

**To hear an in-depth discussion of this Bible account, visit cph.org/podcast and listen to our Seeds of Faith podcast each week.**

## Lesson 8
# Abraham and Isaac
Genesis 21:1–7; 22:1–19

- Copy Student Page 8 for each person.

- For **Opening**, preview the YouTube video in the Old Testament 1 High School playlist at **bit.ly/1knXwnU**. To use it, get equipment ready (e.g., computer, tablet, Internet connection) and cue the video.

  If you do not use the video, hang up a sheet of newsprint (masking tape). Get markers.

- For **God Speaks**, get the Timeline Poster, Bibles, newsprint, masking tape, and markers.

# 1 Opening (10 minutes)

### Fathers and Their Children

**Say** Not everyone has a father in his or her life, but most of us have father figures, men who connect to us and offer time and guidance. This might include older relatives or friends. Think about your father and the father figures in your life. What have you learned from them? Answers vary. If students mention negative qualities, ask them to think about positive influences.

If you use do not use the video, ask students to brainstorm qualities of a good father and write them on the newsprint you hang up. Then skip to the prayer.

If you watch the video, roughly divide your group in half. Ask one half to pay attention to the father's actions. Ask the other half to pay attention to the son.

**Say** Cristiano Ronaldo plays soccer for a Spanish club and for the Portugal national team as the captain. He has won many awards, including the FIFA World Player of the Year Award three times. Often ranked as the best soccer player in the world, Cristiano is raising his son alone.

Show the Lesson 8 YouTube video, "Christiano Ronaldo and Son - A father's story" (3:52; start :09, stop 3:28), in the Old Testament 1 High School playlist at **bit.ly/1knXwnU**.

**Ask** What did you notice about this relationship? How does the father show his love for his son? How does the son show his love for his father? Let students share their observations.

**Pray** Heavenly father, thank You for giving us earthly parents and role models to teach, protect, guide, and love us. Help us to love and respect them as You ask. In Jesus' name we pray. Amen.

# 2 God Speaks (32 minutes)

### A Twenty-Five-Year Wait

**Say** As God promised, Sarah gave birth to Isaac. Let's read about it.

Read **Genesis 21:1–7** aloud, then discuss the following questions.

- **What was God's role in the birth of Isaac?** He worked a miracle in Sarah's old body, allowing her to conceive. It is important to see God's hand in this birth.

▓ **What did Abraham name his son?** Isaac, as God had said to do in Genesis 17:19. Isaac means "laughter," a fitting name since Sarah and Abraham laughed when God said He would give them a son in their old age.

▓ **How do you imagine Abraham and Sarah felt when Isaac was born?** They were certainly joyful and thankful that God had kept His promise. Remind students that Abraham and Sarah had been promised a son many years before and were much too old to conceive a child.

▓ **What did Abraham do to keep his covenant with God?** He circumcised Isaac at eight days old, as God's covenant said. Abraham obeyed God's command.

▓ **How old was Abraham when Isaac was born?** One-hundred years old

▓ **How old was Sarah?** Ninety, ten years younger than Abraham (Genesis 17:17)

▓ **So, at age seventy-five, God brought Abram out of idolatry to follow the living God. The Lord told a childless man He would make him a great nation and bless all the families of the earth through him. Twenty-five years later, God gave him Isaac to begin to fulfill this promise. How do you think waiting twenty-five years changed Abraham?** Abraham's trust in the Lord grew over time. Abraham knew that God kept His Word and that he could trust Him.

## The Test

**Say** Any test can challenge us, such as a chemistry test or a test of courage. Today, we see how Abraham prepared for a test, how he performed during the test, and how God filled in the answers.

Show the Timeline Poster to demonstrate the lesson context.

Hand out Bibles and Student Page 8 copies. Divide into groups of two to five people. If you have fewer students, stay in one group.

Read Student Page directions: **Read Genesis 22 verses, discuss questions, and follow directions.** Students make pictures or word collages to show the relationship between the Lord and Abraham.

Point out the newsprint and markers. Tell students they have twenty minutes to work. As they do so, help as needed and prepare for discussion.

**1–4** **What did God tell Abraham to do?** God gave Abraham the supreme test. He told him to sacrifice his own son Isaac as a burnt offering to God.

**Why does God's request seem bizarre? How does it conflict with the promises God said He would give through Isaac?** God's request to sacrifice Isaac, the long-awaited son, seems incongruent. God promised to establish an everlasting covenant with Isaac and his offspring after him. These are promises of the Messiah.

So, the command to sacrifice Isaac brings questions about God's promises. But God had kept His Word to Abraham, and Abraham trusted God. God never lies. He always keeps His Word. Clearly, this request tested Abraham's faith. Child sacrifice was a detestable practice of the Canaanites who lived around Abraham. God never asked His followers to do this before or since.

**How did Abraham respond?** Abraham did not argue with God. Instead, he obeyed right away. Before Isaac's birth, Abraham tried to get God to substitute Ishmael as the promised son (Genesis 17:18), but God declined. This time, he did not try to substitute Ishmael.

## Key Point

God provided a ram as a sacrifice for Abraham and Isaac. He provides the perfect sacrifice for our sin, His Son, Jesus, the Lamb of God.

## Pronunciations

Beersheba:
    BEAR SHE buh
Moriah:
    moh RYE uh

*Digs into God's Word*

## Key Point

God provided a ram as a sacrifice for Abraham and Isaac. He provides the perfect sacrifice for our sin, His Son, Jesus, the Lamb of God..

**What do you think God wanted to test in Abraham? Why? Read Deuteronomy 13:3; Proverbs 17:3; James 1:2–3 (on Student Page).** God tested Abraham's faith (heart). He wanted to know that Abraham loved Him above all others, even more than his own son Isaac. The other verses illustrate that the Lord tests us to strengthen or steady our faith (steadfastness).

**Who went on the journey?** Abraham, Isaac, two young men

**How long did it take?** Three days

**5–8** **Why did Abraham tell the young men to wait?** He and Isaac would go worship and come back.

**Who carried the wood?** Isaac

**What did Abraham carry?** The fire and the knife

**What did Isaac ask?** Isaac asked where the lamb was for the offering. He was old enough to know that they needed an animal to sacrifice.

**How did Abraham's answer and his actions in these verses show his faith in the Lord?** Abraham said, "God will provide for Himself the lamb." Abraham completely trusted that they would both return to the young men they left behind, that God would provide a lamb for sacrifice.

**9–10** **What did Abraham do to prepare the sacrifice?** Abraham built the altar, laid wood on it, bound Isaac, and laid him on it. He raised the knife to kill Isaac.

**11–19** **What stopped Abraham?** The angel of the Lord called to him from heaven.

**What did the angel of the Lord say?** Not to harm the boy, because He knew that Abraham feared God, since he did not withhold his only son.

**What did God do that fulfilled Abraham's words to Isaac, in verse 8?** He provided the ram for the offering.

**What did the angel of the Lord promise Abraham? Why?** God would bless Abraham and multiply his offspring as the stars in the sky and sand on the seashore. His offspring would control the gates of their enemies and through his offspring (Christ), all the nations of the earth would be blessed.

*Goes to the Heart*

God would do these things because Abraham obeyed His voice and trusted Him, not once but every time He spoke during this narrative.

**Draw a picture or make a word collage that illustrates the relationship between the Lord and Abraham.** Answers vary.

## Debriefing

When time elapses, gather everyone together. Ask groups to hang up their pictures or word collages. Give time for groups to look at everyone's work.

Let students ask questions they may have from the lesson. Especially discuss the second question and the second to last one. Use the answers above to address concerns.

**Say** **Our life stories, like Abraham's, can be viewed from the perspective of faith or unbelief. Whether we approach God with thanks or distrust shows our heart. Many people, including some who claim faith as Christians, blame God for their problems and regard Him and others with distrust.**

**May your trust in the Lord Jesus Christ increase as you grow in grace and knowledge of Him!**

 **3 We Live** (15 minutes)

## The Lamb

**Say** When Isaac asked where to get the sacrifice, Abraham said, "God will provide for Himself the lamb" (Genesis 22:8).

**Their experience points to the greater account of salvation through Christ. Isaac is a type of Christ foreshadowing future events. Let's look at some ways the two correlate.**

Continue with the chart on the Student Page, finding parallels between Isaac and Christ. If students do not know the New Testament corollaries, look them up.

| Abraham/Isaac | | Jesus Christ |
|---|---|---|
| Isaac carried wood for the sacrifice. | See **John 19:17**. | Jesus carried the wood cross for His sacrifice. |
| "Your son, your only son Isaac" (Genesis 22:2) | See **John 3:16**. | God gave up His only Son so those who believe in Him may have life. |
| God will provide the lamb (Genesis 22:8). | See **John 1:29**. | Jesus is the Lamb of God, sacrificed for our sin. |
| Traveled three days, knowing Isaac would die (Genesis 22:4) | See **Matthew 12:40**. | Jesus was buried three days, as He said. |
| Blessings promised to all nations | See **Matthew 28:19–20**. | Jesus said to tell the nations about Him. |

**Say** **God sacrificed His one and only Son for our sins, and He gave us the gift of eternal life through Jesus' death and resurrection.**

**Ask** **How does God test us today?** Discuss possibilities, and be ready to share one of your own. Make sure students are not confused about who passes these tests. By ourselves, we cannot pass. God alone grants us the faith to trust Him. Abraham passed the test because God granted him that certainty and faith.

**The Latin root of the word obey is *oboedire*, which means "to listen to." Did Abraham listen to God? Do we listen to and obey God?** Abraham listened most of the time, but he often failed. We fail to listen to and obey God too. We are, in fact, incapable of obeying God completely, since we are sinful people. Only Jesus Christ kept God's commands perfectly. Through Jesus' suffering, death, and resurrection, we receive eternal life with Him.

 **4 Closing** (3 minutes)

**Say** **What did you learn about God the Father and fathers today?** Thank students who share.

Close by saying the Lord's Prayer together.

*Goes to the Heart*

## Liturgy Link

We sing the *Agnus Dei*, which literally means "Lamb of God," prior to the distribution of Holy Communion. The words reflect the truth that Jesus Christ, the Lamb of God, takes away our sins and grants us peace.

## Faith in Action

Having heard the *Agnus Dei* since childhood, many students may know the words by heart but fail to understand their meaning. Encourage students to listen to the words next time and recall the story of Isaac and the substitutionary sacrifice of the lamb; and to remember God giving Jesus, the Lamb of God, to die on the cross for our sins, and as our substitute.

# Lesson 8
# Abraham and Isaac
Genesis 21:1–7; 22:1–19

## The test

**Directions:** Read **Genesis 22** verses, discuss questions, and follow directions.

### Verses 1–4

▨ What did God tell Abraham to do?

▨ Why does God's request seem bizarre? How does it conflict with the promises God said He would give through Isaac?

▨ How did Abraham respond?

▨ What do you think God wanted to test in Abraham? Why?

> **Deuteronomy 13:3:** The LORD your God is testing you, to know whether you love the LORD your God with all your heart and with all your soul.

> **Proverbs 17:3:** The LORD tests hearts.

> **James 1:2–3:** Count it all joy, my brothers, when you meet trials of various kinds, for you know that the testing of your faith produces steadfastness.

▨ Who went on the journey?

▨ How long did it take?

### Verses 5–8

▨ Why did Abraham tell the young men to wait?

▨ Who carried the wood?

▨ What did Abraham carry?

▨ What did Isaac ask?

▨ How did Abraham's answer and his actions in these verses show his faith in the Lord?

### Verses 9–10

▨ What did Abraham do to prepare the sacrifice?

### Verses 11–19

▨ What stopped Abraham?

▨ Then what did the angel of the Lord say?

▨ What did God do that fulfilled Abraham's words to Isaac, in verse 8?

▨ What did the angel of the Lord promise Abraham? Why?

▨ Draw a picture or make a word collage that illustrates the relationship between the Lord and Abraham.

## The Lamb

| Abraham/Isaac | | Jesus Christ |
|---|---|---|
| Isaac carried wood for the sacrifice. | See **John 19:17**. | |
| "your son, your only son Isaac" (Genesis 22:2) | See **John 3:16**. | |
| God will provide the lamb (Genesis 22:8). | See **John 1:29**. | |
| traveled three days knowing Isaac would die (Genesis 22:4) | See **Matthew 12:40**. | |
| blessings promised to all nations | See **Matthew 28:19–20**. | |

Growing in Christ® High School © 2014, 2016 Concordia Publishing House. Scripture: ESV®. Reproduced by permission.

# Preparing the Lesson

## Isaac and Rebekah

Genesis 24

# Lesson 9

Date of Use

## Key Point

God worked His plan of salvation through the lives of Isaac and Rebekah. God's plan for our salvation is fulfilled through Jesus, their descendant.

## Law/Gospel

God wants me to trust Him for all that I need. **God provides all that I need and gives me forgiveness, life, and salvation through His Son.**

## Context

Abraham and his family, including Isaac, the son of promise, continue to live among the pagan people in the land of Canaan. Abraham, not wanting Isaac to marry one of the Canaanites, charges his oldest servant, unnamed but perhaps Eliezer, to seek a godly wife for Isaac among Abraham's kindred in Mesopotamia.

## Commentary

Abraham entrusts the search for a godly wife for Isaac to a trusted servant. He makes the servant swear not to take a wife for Isaac from the Canaanites. Instead, Abraham sends the servant to bring a wife from the house of Abraham's kindred. The servant wonders whether he should take Isaac back there if the woman will not consent to come back with him.

The faith of Abraham shines forth as he assures the servant that God will send His angel before the servant, making his mission successful. But Abraham knows that even if the woman is not willing to come, Isaac must not leave the land to which God has called Abraham.

The servant departs for the northern region of Mesopotamia, the area around Haran, where Abraham's family first settled after they left Ur of the Chaldeans (Genesis 11:31). The servant bears gifts for the prospective bride and her family, testimonies to the abundant way God has blessed Abraham. The servant asks God to "show steadfast love" (24:12) to Abraham by guiding the servant to the woman He has chosen for Isaac. Before the servant finishes praying, God wonderfully answers the prayer by the appearance of Rebekah, the daughter of Bethuel and granddaughter of Nahor, Abraham's brother. God's abundant grace is further evidenced because Rebekah is also beautiful, a virgin, and very hospitable.

The servant is welcomed into Rebekah's home by her brother Laban with the greeting, "Come in, O blessed of the Lord" (24:31), a greeting that gives testimony to his faith in the Lord. The servant describes how God has blessed his master with great wealth and a son in his old age. He details how the Lord has guided his journey to Rebekah, the one he believes God has chosen to be Isaac's wife.

Rebekah's father and brother agree that indeed "the thing has come from the Lord" (v. 50). Rebekah herself agrees to accompany the servant without delay.

Upon the servant's return, Isaac takes Rebekah to be his wife, and he loves her. From their descendants would be born the Christ, the Bridegroom of the Church. For His Bride, Christ would give His life and cleanse her with the waters of Holy Baptism (Ephesians 5:25–27).

**To hear an in-depth discussion of this Bible account, visit cph.org/podcast and listen to our Seeds of Faith podcast each week.**

Lesson 9

# Isaac and Rebekah

Genesis 24

## Get Ready
### Before Class

- Copy Student Page 9 for each person.

- For **Opening**, preview the YouTube video in the Old Testament 1 High School playlist at **bit.ly/1knXwnU**. To use it, get equipment ready (e.g., computer, tablet, Internet connection) and cue the video.

  If you show the video, post a newsprint sheet with masking tape and get markers.

- For **God Speaks**, get Bibles, the Timeline Poster, paper strips in two different colors, pencils, a bucket or hat, construction paper or newsprint, markers, and masking tape.

 **Opening** (10 minutes)

### Marriage Essentials

When ready to start, stand near the newsprint sheet you hung up.

**Ask**   **Who in your life has been married the longest?** Let students share their experience. If they falter, prompt them with people they may know from church.

**Say**   **Today, we find out how Isaac found a wife. It may be different than any other couple you know.**

If you do not use the video, skip to the opening prayer.

If you show the video, write *Qualities That Make a Strong Marriage* at the top of the newsprint. Recruit two people to serve as scribes and write down qualities mentioned in the video.

**Say**   **This video tells about a couple married for nearly fifty years. Let's see what they think is important for a strong marriage.**

Show the Lesson 9 YouTube video, "That's Amore" (3:15), in the Old Testament 1 High School playlist at **bit.ly/1knXwnU**.

Qualities mentioned include liking each other; saying "I love you"; appreciating each other; serving each other in love (doing everything to make each other happy, such as getting the car while she waits and sharing chores); loving, trusting, and respecting each other; even fighting (knowing each other's strengths and weaknesses but working together); sharing a sense of humor; laughing together; putting God in your marriage; communicating with each other; making each other a priority and spending time together; being best friends; and showing affection.

**Pray**   **Lord God, help us to find mates who love You and share our faith. Help us always to make wise decisions that honor You and show self-respect. In Jesus' name we pray. Amen.**

 **God Speaks** (32 minutes)

### Blind Mate

Divide into two groups. Hand out pencils. Give each group one color of paper strips (two per person). Ask each person in one group to list two positive qualities of a boyfriend or girlfriend on the slips of paper. Ask the other group to list negative qualities.

**Growing in CHRIST**

Give groups about two minutes to work. Fold up, collect, and mix up papers. Ask each person to pick a slip of each color.

**Say**   **Pretend we all decided to let this process choose the perfect spouse for each of us. Read the two characteristics of your future mate.**

Ask all students to read their slip pairs.

**Say**   **You may not like this plan, but in Bible times, as in some cultures today, parents chose spouses for their children. Today's lesson shows a similar plan with all the parts of a modern romance, but in slightly different order.**

**Abraham was 140 years old, and Isaac was 40** (Genesis 25:20)**. What concerns do you think Abraham had at this point in his life?** Let students share ideas, such as his death or wealth distribution.

Hand out Bibles. Recruit volunteers to read **Genesis 24:1–9** as the narrator, Abraham, and the servant, while others follow along.

**Ask**   **So, what was Abraham concerned about? What did he do about it?** Abraham was concerned about getting a wife for Isaac from his own people. He did not want his son to marry a Canaanite. He called his oldest servant to help him find a suitable wife. He made the servant swear not to let Isaac marry a Canaanite, but to go back to his home country and kin to find a suitable mate.

**The servant was probably Eliezer, the person Abraham talked to God about leaving his wealth to before Isaac's birth** (Genesis 15:2)**, but his name is not mentioned here. What did Abraham say his servant could not do?** He could not choose a Canaanite wife for Isaac, but rather from his country and kin. He could not take Isaac away; if the woman wouldn't come, the oath was void.

**Why do you think Abraham didn't want Isaac to marry a local Canaanite?** Abraham had lived among these people for sixty-five years and may have had many reasons. First and foremost, the Canaanites worshiped idols, not the true God. This disparity would make a divided and corrosive marriage.

Abraham's people descended from Noah's son Shem. Noah blessed Shem, but cursed Canaan, his grandson from son Ham. Abraham may not have wanted to be connected to the Canaanite family (Genesis 9:18, 25).

**Say**   **Let's find out what happened with the servant's mission.**

Show the Timeline Poster to demonstrate the lesson context.

Hand out Student Page 9 copies.

Divide into groups of two to five people. If you prefer to do the activity together, have individuals make posters for a group project.

Read Student Page directions: **Read the Genesis 24 verses in your section. Discuss the questions. Make four or more two-word posters to summarize your section for the rest of your group. Add art, if you wish.**

*Digs into God's Word*

Point out the construction paper (or newsprint) and markers. Tell students they have twenty minutes to work. As they do, help as needed and prepare for discussion.

## SECTION ONE

**10–14**   **What did the servant take to Nahor, a city named after Abraham's brother?** Ten camels and choice gifts, most likely for the bride and her family

**What did the servant ask the Lord to do?** Grant him success and show steadfast love to Abraham by showing him Isaac's wife by having her give him a drink and offer to water his camels as well

### Key Point

God worked His plan of salvation through the lives of Isaac and Rebekah. God's plan for our salvation is fulfilled through Jesus, their descendant.

### Pronunciations

Beer-lahai-roi :
    BEE ear-lah HIGH-roy
Bethuel: beh THOO ell
Laban: LAY bihn
Mesopotamia:
    mess oh poh TAME
    ih uh
Milcah: MILL kuh
Nahor: NAY hor

God worked His plan of salvation through the lives of Isaac and Rebekah. God's plan for our salvation is fulfilled through Jesus, their descendant.

**15–21** **Rebekah did exactly what the servant asked God to do as a sign. Camels can drink as much as twenty gallons of water at a time, so watering ten of them would take some time. What did her willingness to help a stranger indicate?** She was hospitable, kind, strong, healthy, hardworking, not shy, and able to meet new people, all positive attributes in a friend and a spouse. She was friendly, kind, not afraid of working, and helpful.

**22–28** **Why did the servant give Rebekah gifts? See also verse 47.** In verse 47, the servant said he gave Rebekah the jewelry after she revealed whose family she belonged to. The nose ring and bracelets thanked Rebekah for her help, honored her, and showed his master's wealth.

**What questions did the servant ask Rebekah? Why were they important?** Asking about her family told the servant if she was related to Abraham; this was important because he was to find a wife for Isaac from Abraham's kin. Asking to stay at her father's home filled a need but also gave the servant the opportunity to ask her father for permission for her to marry Isaac.

### SECTION TWO

**29–32** **Why did Rebekah's brother Laban go out to meet the man?** Laban saw the expensive jewelry, heard the story, and ran to find out more. He may have been curious or excited about the riches and opportunity to meet a connection to his uncle Abraham. He affirmed the invitation to stay at their home.

**How did Laban and his household welcome the servant and his company?** They took care of the camels and fed the servant and men with him.

**33–53** **The servant refused to eat until he told Rebekah's family his story. What stands out to you about his story? In whom did he place his trust?** Answers vary. The servant trusted the Lord God.

**Put the servant's question in verse 49 in your own words.** Answers vary but should include something about asking if Rebekah could marry Isaac.

**How did Rebekah's father Bethuel (Nahor's son) and brother Laban respond?** Seemingly impressed, they acknowledged the Lord's work and would not speak bad or good about it. They agreed that the servant could take Rebekah to become Isaac's wife.

**Goes to the Heart**

**What did the servant do when the family said Rebekah could marry Isaac?** He bowed to the Lord in respect and thanks for the Lord's guidance and help. He also gave gold and silver jewelry and clothing to Rebekah and other gifts to her mother and brother. Although it is not stated here, custom dictated that a bride price be paid as a sign of the covenant, reimbursement for losing the daughter as a worker, and as prepaid alimony in case the husband left his wife. The servant gave Rebekah's mother and brother "costly ornaments."

### SECTION THREE

**54–61** **Rebekah's family acknowledged the Lord's guidance of the servant's mission and gave permission for her to marry Isaac. What happened in the morning?** The servant wanted to leave with Rebekah, but the mother and brother asked that they stay at least ten days. The servant persisted and they called Rebekah, who agreed to go immediately.

**Whom did Rebekah take with her? Also see Genesis 35:8.** She took along her nurse, Deborah, who had raised her from birth, and other young women, probably servants.

**Growing in Christ**

**62–67** **When Rebekah left, she probably never saw her family again. What do you think convinced her to marry Isaac?** She probably had mixed motivations. Surely, the Lord guided her decision. The circumstances likely impressed her as she saw God at work. She also may have liked the gifts and sense of adventure.

**What do you think Isaac meditated about?** He probably prayed or pondered God's promises, wondering if He would fulfill them by finding him a wife.

**What did Rebekah do when she realized the man walking toward them was Isaac? Why?** She covered herself with her veil, as sign of respect, humility, and modesty. We dress up to honor special people and situations. She wanted to put her best foot forward when she met her groom.

**What was the meaning of bringing Rebekah into Sarah's tent?** Since Sarah had died, Rebekah took over Sarah's duties and responsibilities and became the matriarch. She also provided emotional support for the family, comforting Isaac in his grief for his dead mother. This is another reason to marry a spouse who shares our Christian faith, values, and expectations.

**Although this marriage was arranged, what was the outcome?** Isaac loved her. They bonded as husband and wife.

## Debriefing

When time elapses, gather together. Ask groups to show their two-word posters in verse order and tell what happened in their reading. Discuss questions students may have and supplement the discussion with answers provided above.

Ask students to look at Student Page chart. (The next question is not on it.)

**Ask** **How were Rebekah and Isaac related?** Rebekah was Abraham's great-niece, granddaughter of his brother Nahor. This made her Isaac's second cousin.

Haran, father of Abraham's nephew Lot, died before they left Ur (Genesis 11:28).

# ③ We Live (15 minutes)

## Your Love Story

These questions are not on the Student Page so that you can adjust them for your group. You may have students who have had many relationships and others who have never dated. Adjust questions to be appropriate for your group.

**Say** **The story of Isaac and Rebekah is a beautiful love story. Although our dating and marriage customs are different, we can learn some things about finding spouses from this story.**

**Ask** **How was Isaac and Rebekah's relationship different from dating and marriages today?** They did not meet beforehand. They did not choose each other; their families agreed to the union with God's blessing. They did not date, but immediately married. They did not have sexual relations before marriage.

**What is most alien to us about their love story?** Most people object to anyone, especially their families, deciding whom they should marry. The world has convinced people that couples need to ensure compatibility before marrying, including sexual intimacy. Therefore, the world accepts sex before marriage, living together, and informal relationships.

### Faith in Action

Knowing that God desires a husband and a wife to be equally yoked, to share the same faith in Christ (2 Corinthians 6:14), encourage students to pray that God gives them a spouse who shares their faith in our Savior. Tell them they can pray for that person, even now, asking God to protect and guide him or her.

Do not shy away from issues and from presenting God's view of marriage.

Some people marry with divorce as an option if things don't work out. Many break up when they run into conflicts or become attracted to other people. These attitudes may be prevalent in your students or their families.

Many young people have experienced divorce in their families and want to do whatever they can to avoid it. Be sensitive to students who are from divorced families or living-together situations. If someone asks if divorce is a sin, you can say that it may be, but it is one among many.

Jesus said one who divorces for any reason except sexual immorality, and marries another, commits adultery (Matthew 19:3–9). In Bible times, a man could divorce his wife for any reason by setting her property outside the door. She had no recourse, alimony, or claim to household belongings. Jesus said this was wrong.

Jesus said Moses allowed divorce because of the people's hardness of hearts. He quoted Genesis 2:24, "A man shall leave his father and his mother and hold fast to his wife, and they shall become one flesh."

Divorce breaks vows made before God and causes pain in many lives, not just the couple. Adultery, mental and physical abuse, cruelty, and abandonment are also sins. Sometimes the best solution is to leave a hostile, violent setting. This should never happen thoughtlessly, but a couple should seek counseling and reconciliation, if possible.

**Goes to the Heart**

Always, God forgives our sins in Christ Jesus, who wholly committed His life to save ours, suffered and died on the cross to pay for our sins, and rose from the dead to give us a new life, now and forever.

**What did Abraham consider most important in a spouse for Isaac?** Someone who worshiped the true and living Lord.

**Does the Lord want the same for us?** Of course God wants us to have the best, including the blessings of a Christian marriage, built on a foundation of love for God and each other.

**What advantages do you think a marriage has when both people believe in Jesus?** Life decisions challenge our values and beliefs. Christian values are different from those held by nonbelievers and affect what we do with free time, how we raise children, how we spend money, and where we live.

God blesses couples who believe in Him, pray together, and seek God's will for their lives. Worshiping and growing in the grace and wisdom of God increases commitment and strengthens a marriage for good days and troubled times.

## 4 Closing (3 minutes)

**Say** **Name something you learned about marriage today.** Thank students who share.

**In the Lord's Prayer, we pray "give us this day our daily bread." Luther said that this asks God for everything to support and help our bodies, including a devout husband or wife, children, and good friends. As we close with this prayer, silently ask God to be with the spouse He has chosen for you.**

Close by saying the Lord's Prayer together.

**Growing in CHRIST.**

# Lesson 9
# Isaac and Rebekah

Genesis 24

## Blind mate

**Directions:** Read the **Genesis 24** verses in your section. Discuss the questions. Make four or more two-word posters to summarize your section for the rest of your group. Add art, if you wish.

### SECTION ONE

#### Verses 10–14

- What did the servant take to Nahor, a city named after Abraham's brother?

- What did the servant ask the Lord to do?

#### Verses 15–21

- Rebekah did exactly what the servant asked God to do as a sign. Camels can drink as much as twenty gallons of water at a time, so watering ten of them would take some time. What did her willingness to help a stranger indicate?

#### Verses 22–28

- Why did the servant give Rebekah gifts? See also verse 47.

- What questions did the servant ask Rebekah? Why were they important?

### SECTION TWO

#### Verses 29–32

- Why did Rebekah's brother Laban go out to meet the man?

- How did Laban and his household welcome the servant and his company?

#### Verses 33–53

- The servant refused to eat until he told Rebekah's family his story. What stands out to you about his story? In whom did he place his trust?

- Put the servant's question in verse 49 in your own words.

- How did Rebekah's father Bethuel (Nahor's son) and brother Laban respond?

- What did the servant do when the family said Rebekah could marry Isaac?

### SECTION THREE

#### Verses 54–61

- Rebekah's family acknowledged the Lord's guidance of the servant's mission and gave permission for her to marry Isaac. What happened in the morning?

- Whom did Rebekah take with her? Also see **Genesis 35:8**.

#### Verses 62–67

- When Rebekah left, she probably never saw her family again. What do you think convinced her to marry Isaac?

- What do you think Isaac meditated about?

- What did Rebekah do when she realized the man walking toward them was Isaac? Why?

- What was the meaning of bringing Rebekah into Sarah's tent?

- Although this marriage was arranged, what was the outcome?

## Family relationships

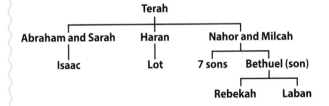

Terah
Abraham and Sarah — Haran — Nahor and Milcah
Isaac — Lot — 7 sons — Bethuel (son)
Rebekah — Laban

# Preparing the Lesson

## Jacob and Esau

Genesis 25:19–34; 27:1–40

## Key Point

God worked through Jacob and Esau, despite their sin, to advance His plan of salvation. In spite of our sinful actions, God accomplishes His will and plan for our lives.

## Law/Gospel

God does not want me to lie and deceive others, but to trust Him and follow His way. **Because of His Son, Jesus, God forgives all my sins and promises to work all things together for my good.**

## Context

Isaac and Rebekah married when Isaac was forty years old. Reminiscent of Abraham and Sarah, almost twenty years later Isaac and Rebekah have no son to be heir of the promise given to Abraham.

## Commentary

Isaac prays to the Lord on behalf of his barren wife, and God enables Rebekah to conceive. As Luther says, "This conception is not the result of the flesh or of nature; God wanted it to take place through the prayer of the saintly patriarch" (Luther's Works 4:343). God's superabundant grace gives not just one son, but two. As the babies struggle in her womb, Rebekah asks God what is happening. He tells her, "Two nations are in your womb," and contrary to custom, "the older shall serve the younger" (Genesis 25:23).

Paul quotes this verse in Romans 9:10–12 to illustrate "God's purpose of election." The firstborn son, Esau, grows up to be a hunter and is beloved by his father, while the younger, Jacob, is a quiet, tent-dwelling man who has captured the affection of his mother.

Perhaps thinking that the birthright of the firstborn son will automatically go to him regardless, Esau one day sells his birthright to Jacob for a bowl of lentil stew. The birthright includes a double portion of the inheritance and the position of family head when the father dies.

Before he dies, Isaac wishes to bless his favored son, Esau. He instructs Esau to hunt game and prepare for him a favorite meal. Unwilling to trust God to fulfill in His own time His promise that Esau would serve Jacob, Rebekah and Jacob scheme to have Jacob impersonate Esau so that Isaac will bless Jacob.

While ingenious, the plan threatens to derail when Isaac questions how quickly the hunter found game and cooked it and then recognizes Jacob's voice. Jacob sins further by saying that God was involved in the nonexistent hunt (Genesis 27:20). But God works His own purposes, allowing Isaac to be deceived. Isaac blesses his son Jacob, granting him an abundance of the necessities of this life, a dominant political kingdom and dominion over his brother, and the blessing given to Abraham that those who bless him will be blessed and those who curse him, cursed (12:3a).

Thus Isaac, thinking he is blessing Esau, tries to reverse what God has said about the older serving the younger. But he stops short of passing along the part of the blessing that promises a Messiah through whom all the families of the earth will be blessed (12:3b). Later, in 28:4, Isaac will knowingly pass on to Jacob the entire blessing given to Abraham.

God's blessing through the patriarch, as Luther says, is no mere wish, but it "states facts and is sure to be fulfilled. . . . It is the bestowal of a good thing" (Luther's Works 5:140). It cannot be revoked. Though Esau pleads with tears, his father has only an inferior blessing for him. God's finest blessing, the blessing of Abraham, goes to Jacob. Through Jacob, God would bless the world with the Savior from sin.

**To hear an in-depth discussion of this Bible account, visit cph.org/podcast and listen to our Seeds of Faith podcast each week.**

Lesson 10

# Jacob and Esau

Genesis 25:19–34; 27:1–40

## Get Ready
### Before Class

- Copy Student Page 10 for each person.

- For **Opening**, preview the YouTube video in the Old Testament 1 High School playlist at **bit.ly/1knXwnU**. To use it, get equipment ready (e.g., computer, tablet, Internet connection) and cue the video.

  Hang up a sheet of newsprint (masking tape). Get markers.

- For **God Speaks**, get Bibles, the Timeline Poster, newsprint, masking tape, and markers.

 **1 Opening** (10 minutes)

### Sibling Rivalry

Gather near the newsprint sheet you hung up.

Ask students to brainstorm a list of things siblings fight over. After one or two minutes, read each item of the list and ask students to vote by raising their hands to say whether they argue about it with their siblings.

**Say**  Today, we meet twins with an incredible story. They fought from the time they were in their mother's womb.

If you do not use the video, skip to the "Say" statement before the prayer.

**Say**  This video shows different twins who also have an incredible story.

Show the Lesson 10 YouTube video, "Surprising Facts About: Twins," (7:26; play 5:58–6:58), in the Old Testament 1 High School playlist at **bit.ly/1knXwnU**.

**Ask**  What surprised you most about these twins? Let students share.

How do you think these strange occurrences happened? Certainly, the facts suggest the men inherited these similarities, but they are truly odd and unexplainable.

**Say**  As we share our lesson, think about your relationships with your own siblings and other family members.

**Pray**  Dear God, You create and keep faith in our hearts. We often turn away and work contrary to Your will. Forgive us, and lead us to a deeper understanding of Your work in our lives. In Christ's name we pray. Amen.

 **2 God Speaks** (37 minutes)

### Brother Bios

Set the stage by showing this lesson on the Timeline Poster.

**Say**  Abraham lived to see the birth of twin sons to Isaac and Rebekah. He had six more sons with a new wife, Keturah, and Ishmael gave him many grandchildren. At 175 years old, God took him home.

Hand out Bibles and Student Page 10 copies. Divide into groups of two to five people. If you prefer to do the activity together, develop profiles of both brothers.

Read Student Page directions: **Read Genesis 25:19–28. On a separate piece of paper, write or draw a biographical sketch of your assigned brother.**

Point out the newsprint and markers. Tell groups they have five minutes to work. As they do, help as needed and review questions to prepare for discussion.

When time elapses, call groups back. Ask students to post their newsprint bios, and give a brief time for them to introduce their brother to the large group.

*Esau:* older twin who struggled in the womb; red and hairy; skillful hunter, outdoorsman; loved by Isaac, who especially enjoyed eating the game caught by Esau; the stronger of the two

*Jacob:* younger twin who struggled in the womb; born holding Esau's heel, so his parents named him Jacob, which means "he takes by the heel" or "he cheats"; loved best by Rebekah; quiet; hung around camp ("dwelling in tents")

Continue with these questions (not on the Student Page).

**Say** **Rebekah was barren, which meant she couldn't have children. You may remember this also was a problem for Sarah, Isaac's mother. What did Isaac ask the Lord to do?** Isaac asked the Lord to give them children.

**What caused Rebekah to "inquire of the LORD"?** The babies struggled within her. Their movements probably made sleeping difficult; she probably worried about the baby's health. She didn't know she had twins.

**What did the Lord tell Rebekah?** She carried two babies, two nations, two divided peoples in her womb. One would be stronger. The older would serve the younger. The information may have made Rebekah favor Jacob.

**The brothers even struggled to be born first.**

**How old was Isaac when the twins were born?** He was sixty, and married twenty years. Abraham was 160 years old.

**Each parent had a favorite son. How do you think this affected the sons?** It probably added to the sibling conflict and gave them more things to argue about. Students may relate similar experiences in their own families.

## A Dysfunctional Family

Recruit a narrator to read **Genesis 25:29–34.** Recruit one person each from the Esau and Jacob groups to read their parts in this Scripture. Encourage them to read in the tone and attitude they think their brother had. Then continue with these questions on the Student Page.

*Digs into God's Word*

**Ask** **How do these verses show the twins' differences?** Esau came home exhausted from working in the fields. Jacob stayed around the tents and cooked. Esau demanded stew, tired and hungry from working all day. Jacob schemed and negotiated while Esau exaggerated his hunger, perhaps to invoke Jacob's pity or guilt. Esau gave in and traded his birthright.

**What was a birthright?** A birthright was the inherited privileges of a firstborn son, which included a double portion of the inherited property, leadership of the family, supervision of worship and preaching of the Messiah, as well as the blessing of becoming the one who carried the covenant promise of the Messiah (*TLSB*, p. 53; 25:31 and 25:34 notes).

**How did Jacob sin?** He felt jealous of his brother. Greed overtook him.

**How did Esau despise his birthright (v. 34)?** Esau treated God's gift carelessly and did not fulfill his responsibilities as oldest son. He may have considered it a joke and didn't think Isaac would enforce the agreement with Jacob because Esau was his favorite. Evidence shows Isaac disregarded it.

## Key Point

God worked through Jacob and Esau, despite their sin, to advance His plan of salvation. In spite of our sinful actions, God accomplishes His will and plan for our lives.

## Pronunciations

Aramean:
    AIR ah MEE un
Edom: EE dum
Esau: EE saw
Paddan-aram:
    PAD uhn-AH rem

## Key Point

God worked through Jacob and Esau, despite their sin, to advance His plan of salvation. In spite of our sinful actions, God accomplishes His will and plan for our lives.

**Who deserved the birthright?** Neither earned or deserved it. It was a gift.

Ask a volunteer to read **Genesis 26:34–35**.

**Ask** **What does this tell us about Esau?** Esau married local idol worshipers. Hittites were foreigners too, from the north and west (modern-day Turkey), but the women's Canaanite names indicate that their families adapted to local culture (*TLSB,* p. 57; 26:34 note). By marrying them, Esau openly defied family expectations and brought idolatry into his home. Polygamy caused many conflicts, and Rebekah sorrowed in dealing with pagan daughters-in-law.

## The Family Meltdown

**Say** **As Isaac aged and became feeble, family conflict continued. Before he died, Isaac planned to give Esau his firstborn blessing, even though Esau had sold his birthright to Jacob.**

*Digs into God's Word*

Move students back into the same small groups. Read the directions on the Student Page: **Read Genesis 27:1–40, discuss the questions, and follow the directions for your assigned brother.**

Let students use the profile newsprint sheets or get new ones, if needed. Give groups fifteen minutes to work.

**The family squabbles came to a logical end. From the perspective of the son you profiled, write why you think Rebekah took action when she overheard Esau and Isaac talking.**

*Esau:* Rebekah acted for Jacob, her favorite son. She helped him steal my birthright. She deceived and defrauded her blind husband and disregarded my firstborn rights.

*Jacob:* Rebekah remembered the Lord's words when she was pregnant, that the older son would serve the younger. She knew Esau sold his birthright and thought I deserved the firstborn blessing. She just "helped" God out.

**In this culture, blessings and curses were irreversible. What did Jacob fear?** He feared Isaac would find out he wasn't Esau and would curse him.

**If you represent Esau, list Rebekah and Jacob's deceptions and lies.** Rebekah schemed with Jacob to get the firstborn blessing for him. She cooked Isaac's favorite meal and sent Jacob to take it to Isaac in Esau's clothing and goat hair. Jacob repeatedly lied to his father.

**If you represent Jacob, list Esau and Isaac's responses to the deceptions.** Isaac trembled very violently as he realized Jacob's deception. Esau cried out with an exceedingly great and bitter cry and begged for his father's blessing. But Isaac had only "leftovers" for Esau.

**Compare the brothers' blessings in verses 27–29 and 39–40. What do you notice about them? Write or draw your brother's blessing.** They are almost opposites of each other.

*To Jacob (disguised as Esau),* Isaac asked God to give the dew of heaven, the fatness of the earth, and plenty of grain and wine. People would serve him; nations would bow down to him. He would lord over his brothers. Everyone who cursed him would be cursed; all who blessed him would be blessed.

*To Esau,* Isaac said his life would be away from the fatness of the earth and dew of heaven. He would live by his sword and serve his brother. But when he grew restless, he would break his brother's yoke from his neck.

**Why do you think Isaac included directions for the family in both blessings?**

**Growing in CHRIST**

**The Hebrew word translated as "your brothers" means all family, including servants.** If Esau had received this blessing as intended, Isaac's favorite would have had control even without his birthright. Instead, Jacob became lord, or boss, as the blessings clarify.

**So, did Esau and Isaac have the right to plot secretly to keep the firstborn blessing? Did Rebekah and Jacob have the right to lie to Isaac and take the blessing from Esau?** Share opinions. All involved sinned, and no one deserved the blessings.

**In the end, what came from all this drama? Read Hebrews 11:20** (on Student Page). Let students share opinions. Isaac gave the blessings in faith. God worked in and through the people. The Messiah came from them.

*Goes to the Heart*

## Debriefing

Tell Esau groups to sit together on one side of the room and Jacob groups on the other. Post the newsprint lists, and use them to review content.

# 3 We Live (10 minutes)

## Look at Us

**Ask** **How are we like Esau and Jacob? Rebekah and Isaac?** Answers vary but should include that we all sin and need God's help and forgiveness. We can let sin and the world drag us down, or we can choose to be positive influences. We can live as forgiven children of God and show God's love in the world. The Holy Spirit works in us and empowers us to do the good works God prepared in advance for us to do (Ephesians 2:10).

**Ask** **In the Lord's Prayer, we ask that God's will be done. How did this family show distrust in God and His will?** They manipulated situations to try to get what they wanted.

**Say** **God wants us to do His will and to trust Him, but we fail. Despite our sin, God works His good in our lives. The Holy Spirit lives in us and helps us.**

**Ask** **How can the following verses encourage us when we feel unworthy or apathetic? when we sin and need forgiveness? Read Romans 8:26–28, 38–39** (on Student Page). Answers vary, but God has given us the Holy Spirit to help in our weakness, to intercede for us, and to bring good out of all things. We can confess our sins and receive forgiveness. Nothing can separate us from God's love in Christ Jesus.

*Goes to the Heart*

# 4 Closing (3 minutes)

**Say** **Name something from the lesson that you never knew before.** Thank students who share.

**God's Word works in our hearts and minds, encouraging us, giving us hope, and assuring us of God's truth and forgiveness in Jesus. What verse that we studied today gives you hope and assurance of God's love?** Thank students who share.

As a closing, read **Romans 8:38–39** aloud together (on the Student Page).

## Faith in Action
Encourage students to have hope, despite situations in their families. Comfort them with the words of **Romans 8.** Suggest they memorize those verses to keep them in their hearts and minds.

# Lesson 10
# Jacob and Esau
Genesis 25:19–34; 27:1–40

## Brother bios

**Directions:** Read **Genesis 25:19–28**. On a separate piece of paper, write or draw a biographical sketch of your assigned brother.

## A dysfunctional family

**Read Genesis 25:29–34.**

- How do these verses show the twins' differences?

- What was a birthright?

- How did Jacob sin?

- How did Esau despise his birthright (v. 34)?

- Who deserved the birthright?

**Read Genesis 26:34–35.**

- What does this tell us about Esau?

## The family meltdown

**Directions:** Read **Genesis 27:1–40**, discuss the questions, and follow the directions for your assigned brother.

- The family squabbles came to a logical end. From the perspective of the son you profiled, write why you think Rebekah took action when she overheard Esau and Isaac talking.

- In this culture, blessings and curses were irreversible. What did Jacob fear?

- If you represent Esau, list Rebekah and Jacob's deceptions and lies.

- If you represent Jacob, list Esau and Isaac's responses to the deceptions.

- Compare the brothers' blessings in verses 27–29 and 39–40. What do you notice about them? Write or draw your brother's blessing.

- Why do you think Isaac included directions for the family in both blessings? The Hebrew word translated as "your brothers" means all family, including servants.

- So, did Esau and Isaac have the right to plot secretly to keep the firstborn blessing? Did Rebekah and Jacob have the right to lie to Isaac and take the blessing from Esau?

- In the end, what came from all this drama?

  **Hebrews 11:20:** By faith Isaac invoked future blessings on Jacob and Esau.

## Look at us

- How are we like Esau and Jacob? Rebekah and Isaac?

- In the Lord's Prayer, we ask that God's will be done. How did this family show distrust in God and His will?

- How can the following verses encourage us when we feel unworthy or apathetic? when we sin and need forgiveness?

  **Romans 8:26–28, 38–39:**
  26 Likewise the Spirit helps us in our weakness. For we do not know what to pray for as we ought, but the Spirit Himself intercedes for us with groanings too deep for words.

  27 And He who searches hearts knows what is the mind of the Spirit, because the Spirit intercedes for the saints according to the will of God.

  28 And we know that for those who love God all things work together for good, for those who are called according to His purpose. . . .

  38 For I am sure that neither death nor life, nor angels nor rulers, nor things present nor things to come, nor powers, 39 nor height nor depth, nor anything else in all creation, will be able to separate us from the love of God in Christ Jesus our Lord.

# Preparing the Lesson

## Jacob's Dream

Genesis 27:41–28:22

Date of Use

## Key Point

God revealed the certainty of His presence now and forever to Jacob in a dream. God reveals Himself and His plan of salvation for us in His Word and Sacraments. We respond with praise and worship.

## Law/Gospel

I sin when I think God does not care for me or has left me alone. **God promises in His Word never to leave me. His gracious love for me, revealed through His Son, Jesus, moves my heart to worship and praise Him.**

## Context

This account shows the consequences of Rebekah and Jacob's deception of Isaac. It also shows how the Lord upholds His children even as they experience the consequences of sin and how He works in their lives and circumstances to accomplish His purposes.

## Commentary

Esau hates Jacob because of the blessing Isaac gave to Jacob, a blessing Esau thinks should have gone to him. When Rebekah hears that Esau plans to kill Jacob, she urges Jacob to go to Laban, her brother, until Esau's anger cools. Rather than tell Isaac about Esau's plot, she instead relates how unhappy she will be if Jacob marries one of the pagan women of the land. Then Isaac directs Jacob to go to Laban and take as a wife one of Laban's daughters. Before sending him on his way, Isaac blesses Jacob with the blessing given to Abraham.

Jacob faces a long, dangerous journey and a painful separation from his parents. Jacob is forced to leave the land that God promised to his grandfather, his father, and now to him. He must take it on faith that God will one day bring him back. But as painful and uncertain as the situation is, God is working in it to provide Jacob with a wife through whom Jacob's greatest descendant, Jesus, would be born.

One night during Jacob's journey, God appears to him in a dream. In the dream, Jacob sees a ladder (or possibly a stairway) set up on earth, with its top in heaven. Angels ascend and descend on the ladder. This dream assures Jacob that God's angels travel from earth to heaven, relaying Jacob's needs to God, and from heaven back to earth to meet those needs.

At the top of the ladder, the Lord Himself appears and reaffirms to Jacob the promises first made to Abraham: that God will give the land of Canaan to Jacob and his offspring, who will be as numerous as dust on the earth, and that through Jacob's offspring all the families on the earth will be blessed. Furthermore, God promises to watch over Jacob and bring him back to this land.

When Jacob awakes, he is awestruck. He marks the place with a pillar, consecrates it, and calls it Bethel, which means "house of God." Then in thanksgiving, he makes a vow to God. Although the vow reveals Jacob's continuing uncertainty about the future, in it he entrusts himself to God's care.

Jesus alludes to Jacob's dream when He says, "Truly, truly, I say to you, you will see heaven opened, and the angels of God ascending and descending on the Son of Man" (John 1:51). As the ladder in Jacob's dream was a bridge between heaven and earth, so Jesus is the ultimate bridge between God and mankind. He is both true God and true man. By His suffering, death, and resurrection, Jesus reconciled sinful humanity to God, and He is the source of eternal blessings for all who trust in Him.

**To hear an in-depth discussion of this Bible account, visit cph.org/podcast and listen to our Seeds of Faith podcast each week.**

# Jacob's Dream

Genesis 27:41–28:22

## Get Ready
### Before Class

- Copy Student Page 11 for each person.

- For **Opening**, preview the YouTube video in the Old Testament 1 High School playlist at **bit.ly/1knXwnU**. To use it, get equipment ready (e.g., computer, tablet, Internet connection) and cue the video.

  Hang up a sheet of newsprint. Set markers nearby.

- For **God Speaks**, get Bibles, the Timeline Poster, and materials for students to use for illustrations, such as newsprint, masking tape, markers, magazines, glue, construction paper, and scissors.

**Goes to the Heart**

## 1 Opening (10 minutes)

### Dreams

Stand by the newsprint sheet you hung up.

**Ask** **What kinds of things stand in the way of you achieving your dreams?** Write responses on the newsprint. Stop after a minute or two.

If you choose not to show the video, continue with the fourth question.

**Say** **You may know YouTube sensation Kid President. What you may not know are some of the barriers he overcomes to follow his dreams.**

Show the Lesson 11 YouTube video, "The True Story of Kid President" (4:22; stop 4:05), in the Old Testament 1 High School playlist at **bit.ly/1knXwnU**.

**Ask** **So what are some of Kid President's dreams and challenges?** Rob's dream is to share hope and joy to make the world a better place. He has osteogenesis imperfecta, a condition that makes his bones break easily. At the time of this video, he had had over seventy breaks and many surgeries. He could easily become discouraged, but instead his joyful, indomitable spirit bubbles over.

**Rob and Brad said, "Wherever you are today, give the world a reason to dance." How would you put their idea into your own words?** Answers vary.

**Kid President said, "Dream with me. . . . What will you create to make the world more awesome?" What kinds of dreams do you have?** Encourage students to share, and be prepared to share yourself.

**How can you expect God to help you achieve your dreams?** God hears and answers our prayers and certainly removes barriers for us. Even more, He brings good out of our mistakes and uses us to serve Him and other people despite our sin. He gives us vocations through which we serve Him, such as son, daughter, sibling, volunteer, and employee.

As Christians, we can live as forgiven children of God and show His love in the world through these vocations. The Holy Spirit works in us and empowers us to do the good works God prepared in advance for us to do (Ephesians 2:10).

**Pray** **Dear Jesus, Your love and forgiveness give us hope and joy. Plant dreams in our hearts and minds that help us discover ways to serve You and to give You glory. In Your holy name we pray. Amen.**

# 2 God Speaks (37 minutes)

## The Meltdown Fallout

**Say** We've been talking about Isaac, Rebekah, and their twin sons, Esau and Jacob. What happened when Isaac blessed his sons? Help those present last week to recall events. Rebekah and Jacob tricked blind Isaac into giving Jacob the firstborn blessing meant for Esau. Esau returned and discovered the treachery. His father blessed him too, but with "leftovers."

**Ask** How do you think Esau felt about Rebekah and Jacob's deceit? Let students speculate. This lesson explores the results of the family dispute.

**When a family goes through an emotional trauma, relationships change and sometimes people experience negative consequences for many years. Let's find out what happened to Rebekah and Isaac's family.**

Show the Timeline Poster to show the lesson context. Hand out Bibles and Student Page 11 copies.

Read Student Page directions aloud: **Read one section and visualize it. Draw a scene, make a word collage or a speech bubble, or chose your own idea. Use the family chart below to help you understand the relationships.**

Divide into groups of two to five people. Assign each one of these parts:

1. **Genesis 27:41**

2. **Genesis 27:42–45**

3. **Genesis 27:46–28:5**

4. **Genesis 28:6–9**

If you have fewer people, assign sections to individuals or do the work as one large group.

Point out supplies. Give students about ten minutes to work. As students work, help as needed and review questions to prepare for discussion.

## Debriefing

When time elapses, bring everyone back together. Ask students to hang up their visuals in verse order. Then, give each group time to explain their drawing and what happened in the verses they read.

Then continue with these questions, which are on the Student Page.

**Ask** Again, Rebekah told Isaac only part of the story. What did she leave out in Genesis 27:46? She did not say that Esau planned to murder Jacob after Isaac died. Instead, she said she did not want Jacob to marry a Hittite woman, which may have been true. She encouraged Isaac to send Jacob away, and he did.

**Before Jacob left, Isaac blessed him again. What blessing did Isaac give that we also receive?** Isaac's blessing included the blessing of Abraham to him and his offspring, the promise of the Messiah.

**How do we receive this blessing? Read Galatians 3:13–14, 27–29** (Student Page). We receive Abraham's blessing through Jesus' death and resurrection, which fulfilled the messianic promise. In Baptism, we put on Christ and are one

### Key Point

God revealed the certainty of His presence now and forever to Jacob in his dream. God reveals Himself and His plan of salvation for us in His Word and Sacraments; we respond with praise and worship.

*Builds Relationships*

### Pronunciations

Hittites: HIT tites

Luz: luhz

Mahalath:
　　MAY huh lath

Nebaioth:
　　neh BUY yoth

with Him. Since we belong to Him, we also are Abraham's offspring and heirs of God's promise to bless all nations through Christ Jesus.

**How did Esau try to please his father?** Esau heard Isaac sent Jacob away so he wouldn't marry a Canaanite woman. Realizing his wives were Canaanites, Esau found an Ishmaelite woman to marry, a granddaughter of Abraham.

**Jacob received the birthright and the blessing of his father, but he had to run from his brother's rage and did not return for twenty years. He left behind his family and all the belongings he received in the birthright. Why do you think this happened?** Let students discuss ideas. Help them know God worked through this family despite their sin to bring His Son into the world.

**Martin Luther said this trial tested Jacob to see if he'd cling to the blessing in faith and wait. "If God did not test us and postpone His promises, we would not be able to love Him wholeheartedly. For if He immediately gave everything He promises, we would not believe but would immerse ourselves in the blessings that are at hand and forget God"** (AE 5:202). **Do you agree or disagree?** Let students discuss various viewpoints.

**What dangers and challenges could someone encounter while traveling and in a foreign land?** Traveling alone made Jacob easy prey to robbers. He didn't know anyone. Eventually, he'd have to ask family members he never met for food, clothing, and shelter. He'd experience different laws and customs.

## Jacob's Dream

**Digs into God's Word**

Let students go back into their same small groups. Give students ten to fifteen minutes to read **Genesis 28:10–22** and discuss these Student Page questions.

**12** **What gift did God give Jacob to reassure him that he was not alone?** God gave Jacob a dream. In it, he saw a ladder with angels ascending and descending from heaven.

**13–15** **What did the Lord promise Jacob?** The Lord appeared above the ladder and promised to be with Jacob always. God reassured Jacob he would return to his homeland, and He repeated the messianic blessing of Abraham that he would have offspring like the dust of the earth. God would bless all the earth's families through Jacob and his offspring, the Christ.

**Goes to the Heart**

**What gifts does God give us to reassure us that we are not alone?** God places us in a community of believers in Christ, and He gives family and friends who love us. God gives us His Word and strengthens our faith through Holy Communion, sharing His real body and blood, His real presence, with us.

**What do you think the dream meant? Read John 1:51** (Student Page)**.** The dream assured Jacob that God was with him, but it also showed that Christ would descend to earth. In John 1:51, Jesus compared Himself to the ladder. He is the way that God came to us and the way we return to God (John 14:6).

**16–17** **What did Jacob do when he woke?** He felt awed and afraid. He called the place "the house of God" and "the gate of heaven."

**18–19** **How did Jacob mark the place of the dream?** He set up the stone he slept on as a pillar. He poured oil on it to consecrate it as a holy place. He named it Bethel ("house of God," the place where God dwells).

**20–22** **What vow did Jacob make?** If God would be with him and take care of his needs (bread, clothing) so that he would return to his father's house in peace, then the Lord would be his God and this stone would be God's house. He would give a tenth of his wealth to the Lord.

Bring students back together. Discuss together the questions for **verses 13–15**. As time permits, discuss other questions students have.

# 3 We Live (10 minutes)

## The Fear of the Lord

Continue in your large-group discussion. These questions are not on the Student Page, but the Scripture verse is.

**Say** **Martin Luther liked the narrative of Jacob's ladder because it is good "for us to hear of the weaknesses of the saints" (AE 5:254). What do you think Luther meant? Do you agree or disagree? Why?** Luther went on to say he knew he couldn't imitate heroics like David killing Goliath. "But when examples of weakness, sins, trepidation, and trials are set forth in the saints . . . they buoy me up. . . . For I see how they, fearful and terrified though they were, did not perish but buoyed themselves up with the promises they had received; and from this I conclude that there is no need for me to despair either."

**Has God ever made you wait for an answer to prayer? Did you get impatient and give up?** Answers vary. Many people in the Bible waited for God to keep His promises, from the time God promised a Savior to Adam and Eve to the time the Savior was born in a stable in Bethlehem thousands of years later.

**How can knowing that God sometimes waits years to answer our prayers comfort us?** It helps us learn to be patient and trust in the Lord.

**How does God work in our lives as He did Jacob's?** God acts in our lives as He did in Jacob's. Through His Word and in Baptism, God reaches out with love, grace, and forgiveness in Christ Jesus, His Son and our Lord. The Holy Spirit guides, protects, nurtures, and keeps us in the one true faith through His Word and Sacraments.

**How and why should we fear the Lord? Read Proverbs 1:7 (Student Page).** We fear the Lord when we understand that He is holy and perfect, the Creator of the universe, and beyond our comprehension. In comparison, we realize that we are poor, miserable sinners who need His grace and forgiveness. Fools trust themselves and despise the Lord and His teachings.

*Goes to the Heart*

# 4 Closing (3 minutes)

**Say** **Finish this sentence: Something I want to learn more about is . . . .** Thank students who share.

**Pray** **Lord God, You revealed Your presence to Jacob in a dream. You reveal Yourself and our Savior in Your Word and Sacraments. Thank You for the privilege to hear and taste God's goodness through Jesus Christ, Your only Son and our Lord. Amen.**

## Faith in Action

Ask students to think of ways they can show God's love, mercy, and forgiveness to their parents, siblings, and other relatives. Read the Fourth Commandment and its meaning from Luther's Small Catechism. Discuss how they can honor and respect their parents. Talk about ways to honor and respect all family members.

# Lesson 11
# Jacob's dream

Genesis 27:41–28:22

## The meltdown fallout

**Directions:** Read one section and visualize it. Draw a scene, make a word collage or a speech bubble, or chose your own idea. Use the family chart below to help you understand the relationships.

1. **Genesis 27:41**
2. **Genesis 27:42–45**
3. **Genesis 27:46–28:5**
4. **Genesis 28:6–9**

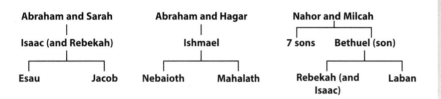

Abraham and Sarah — Isaac (and Rebekah) — Esau, Jacob

Abraham and Hagar — Ishmael — Nebaioth, Mahalath

Nahor and Milcah — 7 sons, Bethuel (son) — Rebekah (and Isaac), Laban

## Debriefing

- Again, Rebekah told Isaac only part of the story. What did she leave out in **Genesis 27:46**?

- Before Jacob left, Isaac blessed him again. What blessing did Isaac give that we also receive?

- How do we receive this blessing?

   **Galatians 3:13–14:** Christ redeemed us from the curse of the law by becoming a curse for us . . . so that in Christ Jesus the blessing of Abraham might come to the Gentiles, so that we might receive the promised Spirit through faith.

   **Galatians 3:27–29:** For as many of you as were baptized into Christ have put on Christ. There is neither Jew nor Greek, there is neither slave nor free, there is no male and female, for you are all one in Christ Jesus. And if you are Christ's, then you are Abraham's offspring, heirs according to promise.

- How did Esau try to please his father?

- Jacob received the birthright and the blessing of his father, but he had to run from his brother's rage and did not return for twenty years. He left behind his family and all the belongings he received in the birthright. Why do you think this happened?

- Martin Luther said this trial tested Jacob to see if he'd cling to the blessing in faith and wait. "If God did not test us and postpone His promises, we would not be able to love Him wholeheartedly. For if He immediately gave everything He promises, we would not believe but would immerse ourselves in the blessings that are at hand and forget God" (AE 5:202).

- Do you agree or disagree?

- What dangers and challenges could someone encounter while traveling and in a foreign land?

## Jacob's dream

**Read Genesis 28:10–22.**

- What gift did God give Jacob to reassure him that he was not alone?

- What did the Lord promise Jacob?

- What gifts does God give us to reassure us that we are not alone?

- What do you think the dream meant?

   **John 1:51:** [Jesus said,] "Truly, truly, I say to you, you will see heaven opened, and the angels of God ascending and descending on the Son of Man."

- What did Jacob do when he woke?

- How did Jacob mark the place of the dream?

- What vow did Jacob make?

## The fear of the Lord

   **Proverbs 1:7:** The fear of the LORD is the beginning of knowledge; fools despise wisdom and instruction.

# Preparing the Lesson

## Jacob's Family

Genesis 29:1–30:24

### Key Point

Through Jacob's family, God brought forth the Savior, Jesus Christ, who endured lies, deception, and the schemes of sinful mankind to work our salvation on the cross.

### Law/Gospel

I sin when I lie or deceive others. **In spite of my sin, God blesses me with my family and all that I need and forgives me for the sake of His own Son, Jesus.**

### Context

Jacob, with the aid of his mother, Rebekah, had deceived his twin brother, Esau, and his father, Isaac. Because Esau was so angry with him, Rebekah, afraid for Jacob's life, convinced Isaac to send him to his uncle Laban (Rebekah's brother) to find a wife. On the journey, God came to Jacob in a dream, renewing the threefold promise that He had previously made with Abraham (Genesis 12:3; 28:14).

### Commentary

The deceiver was deceived. After Jacob deceived his father and brother, his uncle Laban deceived him in marriage. Jacob did not get the bride of his choosing until he promised to work for another seven years.

Jacob loves Rachel more than Leah. This causes competition within the marriage. Jacob fulfills his marital duty with Leah only out of obligation. Despite this jealousy, God intercedes and works His will. Leah becomes the mother of Jacob's sons. One of her sons will be the father of God's line of priests; another will be the father of King David and ultimately of Jesus Christ. Leah is blessed. God looks upon the oppressed and distraught and gives blessings without measure. Leah's dishonor as the "unloved" wife is overshadowed and vanquished by the lineage of the Messiah.

It is now Rachel's turn to feel dishonored. Barrenness is a heavy cross for a woman to bear. Barrenness excludes Rachel from participating in creation's ordinance of being fruitful and multiplying. It also excludes her from God's promise to Eve that a woman would bear the Seed that will crush the serpent's head. Her husband loves her, but she is not able to produce the fruit of that love. By God's grace, however, Rachel receives an answer to her prayer and gives birth to Joseph and Benjamin, Jacob's favorite sons.

Laban's sinful deception, Jacob's sinful favoritism, and the sisters' sinful jealousy and competition are unable to thwart God's promise. God works His good. The family of Abraham expands. The twelve tribes of Israel wait only for the birth of Benjamin. God's course of action is never derailed because of the sinfulness of His people. Nothing can stop His love. The world will be blessed through this family despite their past, present, and future sinfulness. Despite the insurmountable odds, God would become man through Abraham's family. Jesus would live, suffer, and die even for the sins of His ancestors.

**To hear an in-depth discussion of this Bible account, visit cph.org/podcast and listen to our Seeds of Faith podcast each week.**

# Lesson 12
# Jacob's Family
Genesis 29:1–30:24

## Get Ready
### Before Class

- Copy Student Pages 12A and 12B for each person.

- For **Opening**, write *deception* on a sheet of newsprint or on the board. Get index cards and pencils or pens.

- For **God Speaks**, preview the YouTube video in the Old Testament 1 High School playlist at **bit.ly/1knXwnU**. To use it, get equipment ready (e.g., computer, tablet, Internet connection) and cue the video.

  Get Bibles, the Timeline Poster, pencils or pens, newsprint, markers, and masking tape.

- For **We Live**, use the *deception* sign from Opening.

## 1 Opening (10 minutes)

### Deception

Hand out index cards; ask students to write three statements about themselves, two true statements and one false statement. Encourage them to be creative. Example: I have never eaten pizza. I love classical music. I am allergic to antibiotics.

Take turns reading statements aloud, reminding students to read each one with conviction. After each card reading, ask the class to vote on which statement is false.

If your class is large, work in smaller groups to speed up the activity and to help shy students with their discomfort about speaking in front of a large group.

After all have shared, point out the *deception* sign. Discuss how difficult it is to determine the truth when someone determines to deceive you.

**Say**  Today, we learn more about Jacob, the younger one of Isaac's twin sons. His name can have a couple of different meanings, including "he cheats" or "deceiver." Let's find out how God used this sinner in His plan of salvation.

**Pray**  Dear Lord, bless our time together in Your Word. Guide our thoughts and our discussions as we learn more about Your promises to us. Forgive us and renew us in Jesus, our Lord and Savior. In His name we pray. Amen.

## 2 God Speaks (37 minutes)

### Jacob Arrives in Haran

Show the Timeline Poster to demonstrate the lesson context. Hand out Bibles.

**Say**  You may remember that Jacob left his family because his brother, Esau, planned to kill him and because his mother, Rebekah, wanted him to marry someone from her family, not a Canaanite woman. Rebekah sent Jacob to Haran, her hometown where her brother Laban lived.

Ask volunteers to read **Genesis 29:1–14** as a narrator (or two), Jacob, two or more shepherds, and Laban.

**Say**  Remember, people then couldn't communicate by social media, text, phone, or letter. This was probably the first time Laban heard any news about his sister and her family. Do any social customs seem odd to you? Students may mention kissing relatives, Jacob publicly weeping, or running to greet a visitor.

**Growing in CHRIST.**

**What new information do these verses give us about Jacob?** Students may mention his emotions or his strength. He moved the stone from the well by himself when the shepherds waited for everyone to help.

If you choose not to show the video, continue with Life with Laban.

**Say**  **Jacob may have felt alone, but God was with him. He found family members in Haran and eventually had a family with at least thirteen children. It may be difficult for us to understand life in a family this large. Look for advantages and disadvantages in this video.**

Show the Lesson 12 YouTube video, "The Radford Family | Where You Belong" (2:00), in the Old Testament 1 High School playlist at **bit.ly/1knXwnU**.

**Ask**  **What did you see as some positives or negatives in this large family?** They mourn, celebrate, play, and work together. Everyone helps with chores. They argue, but also work to get along and love one another. Students may mention other concerns, such as space, privacy, jealousy, and costs.

**Say**  **Keep these things in mind as we find out about Jacob's family.**

## Life with Laban

Divide into groups of two to five people. Assign each group a wife: Leah, Rachel, Bilhah, or Zilpah.

If you choose to keep your group together, draw crests for one or more wives.

Hand out copies of Student Pages 12A and 12B. Read the directions on Student Page 12A: **Read the Scripture verses and discuss the questions. As you do, fill in the family chart on Student Page 12B. Draw a family crest to represent your assigned wife and her children.**

Point out the newsprint and markers. Tell groups they have twenty minutes to discuss all questions to work. As students work, help as needed and review questions to prepare for discussion.

**Genesis 29:15–30**

**Why did Jacob love Rachel?** She was beautiful. The Bible says Leah had "weak" eyes, probably a description of her lack of beauty.

**To marry Rachel, Jacob served Laban for seven years. In their culture, the groom or his family paid a bride price to finalize a marriage contract. The payment usually involved material goods, but it could involve service, as in Jacob's case.**

**How did Laban deceive Jacob?** Laban gave Leah to Jacob on the evening of the wedding feast instead of Rachel. Students may question how this could happen. The evening was probably followed with a festival with much drinking; it was dark; and Leah was probably veiled, as was the custom for weddings.

**It is ironic that Laban deceived Jacob, who deceived his father and brother. Jacob's name means "he cheats" or "deceiver." Why do you think God permitted this deception?** God had great plans for Jacob and his family. God didn't hold Jacob's sin against him. God forgave Jacob, but the consequences of his sin lingered.

**What quality did Jacob exhibit when he agreed to serve Laban for another seven years to marry Rachel?** Patience. Jacob's disappointment was great. We might expect him to demand that Laban give him Rachel, since that was the formal agreement. However, Jacob submitted humbly to Laban and served him

### Key Point
Through Jacob's family, God brings forth the Savior, Jesus Christ, who endured lies, deception, and the schemes of sinful humankind to work our salvation on the cross.

*Digs into God's Word*

### Pronunciations
Bilhah: BILL hah
Issachar: IHZ ah car
Naphtali: NAF tuh lee
Reuben: ROO ben
Zebulun: ZEBB you lun
Zilpah: ZILL pah

Through Jacob's family, God brings forth the Savior, Jesus Christ, who endured lies, deception, and the schemes of sinful humankind to work our salvation on the cross.

**Goes to the Heart**

for seven more years. Rachel became his bride a week later, when the formal first week with wife Leah passed.

### Genesis 29:31–30:24; 35:16–18

**As you read, list on Student Page 12B the names of the wives and children. Check Bible footnotes to find meanings of the children's names and jot them down, especially for your assigned wife. Use this information in your family crest.**

From left to right on the chart: **Leah** birthed Reuben (see, a son), Simeon (heard), Levi (attached), Judah (praise), Issachar (wages, hire), Zebulun (honor), and Dinah (no meaning given).

**Bilhah,** Rachel's servant, had Dan (judged) and Naphtali (wrestling).

**Zilpah,** Leah's servant, had Gad (good fortune) and Asher (happy).

**Rachel** had Joseph (may He add) and Benjamin (son of the right hand).

**How did God use even the sinful, bitter jealousies of the sisters to fulfill His promise?** The competition between Leah and Rachel was fierce and bitter, but the Lord continued to bless the family with children. Leah's fourth son, Judah, gives the Jewish people their name. Through Judah, Leah became an ancestor of King David and of the Messiah Himself.

### Debriefing

When time elapses, call everyone back together and ask groups to hang up their family crests. Let each group give reasons for what they added to the crests.

As time permits, you might discuss why God allowed Jacob to marry more than one woman. This is not God's will for His people. God's plan for marriage in Genesis 1 includes one man and one woman. Encourage students to discuss times they witnessed conflict between friends who loved the same person.

## **3 We Live** (10 minutes)

### Because of the Cross of Christ

Questions are not listed on the Student Page, but the parts of the catechism are.

**Say**   **It's easy to read about Jacob's family and judge their behavior. The truth is that we live sinful lives of deception, lies, jealousy, and anger too. What is deception?** Deception is when someone purposefully tries to lead someone else to believe a partially true or totally untrue statement or circumstance.

**When do we try to deceive?** Encourage students to think about times they deceived someone. Encourage them to recognize common deceptions in our world. For example, teens are masters of half-truths. They might also mention ads, news broadcasts, and situations they experienced.

**Say**   **Thank God for His gift of forgiveness through the work of Christ on the cross! Let's read the Second Article of the Apostles' Creed and its explanation from Luther's Small Catechism** (Student Page).

**Ask**   **What blessing do we have because of Jesus Christ?** Write *redemption* on the *deception* sign from Opening. Cross out *deception*.

**What is redemption?** Redemption is being freed or bought back from the price of our sin; it's why God's Son came to earth. Jesus took on flesh, lived without

## Faith in Action

Tell students to remember God's grace in Christ the next time they confront deception and sin, which could happen every day for some students. Encourage them to speak the truth in love (Ephesians 4:15) and forgive as God in Christ forgives us (Ephesians 4:32).

**Goes to the Heart**

sin, but suffered and died on the cross to pay for our sins, redeeming us with His blood. Then God raised Christ from the dead and claimed victory over death and the devil. We receive the gift of redemption by grace through faith in Christ our Savior, delivered by the Holy Spirit to us through God's Word and Sacraments.

**Why did Jesus have to suffer and die?** In the Garden of Eden, humans sinned and broke the perfect relationship between God and people. Once sin entered the world, it infected all humans; death and self-destruction followed. Our sinful nature made us enemies of our holy, perfect God (Romans 5:10). We could not save ourselves.

God sent His Son, Jesus, into the world to reconcile us with Him. Jesus, the sinless one, paid for our sins on the cross. He rose from the dead to give us new life, now and forever. We receive faith and the benefits of Jesus' work through Baptism, where we are united in His death and resurrection (Romans 6:3–11).

**Do unbelievers receive this blessing?** No, only those who believe that Jesus Christ's death and resurrection purchased our sins forever have it. Ultimately, unbelievers lose blessings for an eternity unless they come to faith.

**What does Jacob have to do with Christ's death and resurrection?** Jacob was a sinner, just as we are. Yet he lived and died as a redeemed child of God because of the promise of the Messiah, who descended from Judah, son of Jacob and Leah. God's salvation plan through the Messiah could not be stopped even by humankind's deception, lies, jealousies, or selfishness.

**Say** **Despite the sinfulness of Jacob's family, God blessed the world through them in Christ Jesus, our Savior.**

## Key Point

Through Jacob's family, God brings forth the Savior, Jesus Christ, who endured lies, deception, and the schemes of sinful humankind to work our salvation on the cross.

*Goes to the Heart*

# (4) **Closing** (3 minutes)

**Say** **Finish this sentence: The best thing about being part of God's family is . . . .** Thank students who share.

**Pray** **Heavenly Father, help us discern words of truth and deception. Help us speak the truth in love and also speak about the sacrificial love You showed by sending Your Son, Jesus Christ, to die on the cross for our sins. Strengthen us to respond to Your love with our obedience, praise, and service for Christ's sake. Amen.**

# Lesson 12
# Jacob's family

Genesis 29:1–30:24

## Life with Laban

**Directions:** Read the Scripture verses and discuss the questions. As you do, fill in the family chart on Student Page 12B. Draw a family crest to represent your assigned wife and her children.

### Read Genesis 29:15–30.

▨ Why did Jacob love Rachel?

To marry Rachel, Jacob served Laban for seven years. In their culture, the groom or his family paid a bride price to finalize a marriage contract. The payment usually involved material goods, but it could involve service, as in Jacob's case.

▨ How did Laban deceive Jacob?

▨ It is ironic that Laban deceived Jacob, who deceived his father and brother. Jacob's name means "he cheats" or "deceiver." Why do you think God permitted this deception?

▨ What quality did Jacob exhibit when he agreed to serve Laban for another seven years to marry Rachel?

### Read Genesis 29:31–30:24, 35:16–18.

▨ As you read, list the names of the wives and children on Student Page 12B. Check Bible footnotes to find the meanings of the children's names and jot them down, especially for your assigned wife. Use this information in your family crest.

▨ How did God use even the sinful, bitter jealousies of the sisters to fulfill His promise?

## The Second Article of the Apostles' Creed: Redemption

[I believe] in Jesus Christ, His only Son, our Lord, who was conceived by the Holy Spirit, born of the Virgin Mary, suffered under Pontius Pilate, was crucified, died and was buried. He descended into hell. The third day He rose again from the dead. He ascended into heaven and sits at the right hand of God, the Father Almighty. From thence He will come to judge the living and the dead.

***What does this mean?*** I believe that Jesus Christ, true God, begotten of the Father from eternity, and also true man, born of the Virgin Mary, is my Lord,

who has redeemed me, a lost and condemned person, purchased and won me from all sins, from death, and from the power of the devil; not with gold or silver, but with His holy, precious blood and with His innocent suffering and death,

that I may be His own and live under Him in His kingdom and serve Him in everlasting righteousness, innocence, and blessedness,

just as He is risen from the dead, lives and reigns to all eternity.

This is most certainly true.

# Jacob's Family

Wife

_____

_____

_____

_____

_____

_____

_____

_____

Servant

_____

_____

_____

Servant

Wife

_____

_____

_____

# Preparing the Lesson

## Esau Forgives Jacob

Genesis 31:3; 32–33

## Key Point

Though Jacob was sinful and deceived his brother, God preserved his life and reconciled him with his brother, Esau. Through His Son, God preserves our lives. Jesus overcame sin and death on the cross to win our forgiveness, life, and salvation.

## Law/Gospel

Broken families and failed friendships are the result of sin. **Jesus' forgiveness restores my broken relationship with God and can heal my broken earthly relationships as well.**

## Context

God blessed Jacob with a large family and many earthly possessions while he lived and worked with Laban. At God's command, Jacob leaves his father-in-law and starts for the land of his fathers—the land of promise. Fearing Laban's wrath, Jacob flees with all that God has given him.

Because Jacob left in secret and Rachel stole her father's idols, Laban pursues Jacob. When Laban overtakes Jacob's group, the two discuss Jacob's departure and search in vain for the stolen idols. Jacob decries the unfair manner of Laban's treatment of him. They make a covenant together, and Jacob departs for the Promised Land with Laban's blessing.

## Commentary

When Esau hears that Jacob is coming back, he gathers a group of four hundred men to meet Jacob. In his distress, Jacob prays for the Lord's intervention and help (Genesis 32:9–12). Jacob respeaks God's words into His ears. He reminds God of the promise of land and innumerable descendants He gave to his grandfather Abraham, to his father, Isaac, and to him.

God hears Jacob's prayer for deliverance and comes to wrestle with Jacob. Jacob limps away from this encounter, but not without first receiving a new name and a divine blessing. Jacob grappled with man in the womb (25:22, 26) for the family birthright. Now he struggles with God for a heavenly birthright. Israel ("God's fighter") is the name given to Jacob. It will become the coat of arms for the tribes of his twelve sons, who will be heirs of a heavenly birthright, struggling with both men and God.

The crown of Israel is the struggle between God and man in the person of the God-man, Jesus Christ. In Jesus, God struggles with men. Even more, He struggles for men. God's cosmic struggle for mankind does not end with a sore hip, but rather with a bruised heel (3:15).

The name of God is not yet revealed to Jacob. However, Jacob knows that God struggled with him, for God says, "You have striven with God and with men" (32:28). Jacob renames the place of this encounter Peniel ("the face of God"). Now, Esau meets Jacob not for war, but for peace.

**To hear an in-depth discussion of this Bible account, visit cph.org/podcast and listen to our Seeds of Faith podcast each week.**

# Esau Forgives Jacob

Genesis 31:3; 32–33

## Get Ready

**Before Class**

- Copy Student Page 13 for each person

- For **Opening**, preview the YouTube video in the Old Testament 1 High School playlist at **bit.ly/1knXwnU**. To use it, get equipment ready (e.g., computer, tablet, Internet connection) and cue the video.

  Get half sheets of paper and pencils or pens.

- For **God Speaks**, get Bibles, the Timeline Poster, newsprint, markers, and masking tape.

## 1 Opening (10 minutes)

### Thankful Living

Hand out pieces of paper and pencils or pens.

**Say** **Write a list of ten things you feel thankful for.** Tell students they don't have to share the list unless they want to. Give students a minute to make their list.

If you choose not to show the video, go to the second question.

**Say** **You may remember Kid President. Today, Kid President shares some things for which he feels thankful.**

Show the Lesson 13 YouTube video, "Kid President's 25 Reasons To Be Thankful!" (3:47; stop 3:10), in the Old Testament 1 High School playlist at **bit.ly/1knXwnU**.

**Ask** **Did Kid President list anything you'd like to add to your list?** Encourage discussion of the video list and the lists students made.

**How does it help us to list things we feel thankful for?** Listing our blessings makes us pause and consider God's goodness to us. It puts our emphasis on what God has done for us and the blessings we enjoy instead of negatively focusing on wanting bigger, better, or more.

**Pray** **Lord God, thank You for all the gifts You give that nurture and preserve our bodies, minds, and souls. Thank You especially for sending Jesus as our Savior. Open our hearts to Your Word. In Jesus' name we pray. Amen.**

## 2 God Speaks (32 minutes)

### Journey to Reconciliation

**Say** **Today, we explore the life of Jacob, son of Isaac and Rebekah, younger twin of Esau. You may remember that the twins became estranged when their mother plotted to get the firstborn blessing for her favorite, Jacob.**

**Jacob ran away because Esau planned to kill him. Who can tell what happened to Jacob then?** Help students recall that Rebekah sent Jacob to her brother Laban, over seven hundred miles away in Haran. There, Jacob fell in love with Laban's daughter Rachel. He worked seven years to marry her, but Laban tricked him and gave him his older daughter Leah instead.

Jacob worked another seven years to marry Rachel. Leah, Rachel, and their two servants became tangled in a jealous rivalry that resulted in the birth of twelve sons and at least one daughter.

**Growing in CHRIST.**

Hand out Bibles and ask students to turn to **Genesis 31**.

**Say**  **After Jacob worked fourteen years for his wives, Laban begged him to stay and negotiated wages. God blessed Jacob, and through him, Laban became very wealthy, even though he constantly tried to cheat Jacob.**

**After six more years, Laban's sons accused Jacob of stealing, and he realized Laban no longer favored him. The Lord sent Jacob a message.**

Ask a volunteer to read **Genesis 31:3**.

**Ask**  **What did the Lord promise Jacob?** The Lord promised to be with him, just as He earlier promised in Jacob's dream when he left home (Genesis 28:15).

**What do you think Jacob worried about when God told him to go home?** Let students anticipate Jacob's worry about how Laban would take the news (31:20) and his fear of Esau (32:1–8). Jacob also probably worried about how to travel that distance safely with his wives, children, and flocks.

**Jacob decided to sneak away with his family, but Laban pursued him. Laban made a covenant with Jacob, kissed his daughters and grandchildren, and went home. This is where our lesson starts.**

Show the Timeline Poster to demonstrate the lesson context.

Divide into groups of two to five people. Let each group choose to do Part 1, **Genesis 32**, or Part 2, **Genesis 33**.

Read Student Page directions: **Read your assigned verses, discuss questions, and follow directions.** Part 1 groups visualize the present parade. Part 2 groups write social media posts to report the events.

If you choose to keep your group together, hang up two sheets of newsprint and do both activities together.

Point out the newsprint and markers. Tell groups they have fifteen or twenty minutes to work. Help as needed and review questions to prepare for discussion.

### Part 1: Genesis 32

**1–2**  **What did the angels' presence tell Jacob?** God was with him as promised (31:3). Angels guided and protected Jacob and his family.

**3–8**  **How did Jacob decide to approach Esau?** He sent messengers to tell Esau he was returning with animals and servants. He did not mention his family.

**What did Esau say in response? What did Jacob think and do about this?** Esau sent back word that he would come meet him with four hundred men. Jacob took this as a threat. He felt very afraid and upset. Jacob divided his family into two camps so if one was attacked, the other would escape.

**9–12**  **Find a main message in each verse of Jacob's prayer to the Lord.** Verse 9: You told me to go home. Verse 10: I am not worthy of Your love, faithfulness, and great blessings (confession). Verse 11: Help me. I feel afraid for me and my family. I need Your help. Verse 12: Remember Your promises to me.

**13–24**  **What present did Jacob decide to give his brother Esau?** Two hundred female goats and ewes, twenty male goats, twenty rams, thirty milking camels and their calves, forty cows, ten bulls, twenty female donkeys, ten male donkeys.

**What strategy did Jacob use to offer the present?** He separated the animals into individual groups and sent them ahead. When Esau met them, Jacob told his servants to say to Esau that the animals now belong to him, as a present.

## Key Point

Though Jacob was sinful and deceived his brother, God preserved his life and reconciled him with his brother, Esau. Through His Son, God preserves our lives. Jesus overcame sin and death on the cross to win our forgiveness, life, and salvation.

*Digs into God's Word*

## Pronunciations

El-Elohe-Israel:
    el-eh LOW heh-
    IS ray ell
Hamor: HAY mohr
Mahanaim:
    may huh NAY im
Peniel: PEN ih ehl
Penuel: PEN you uhl
Seir: SEE ur
Succoth: SUK oth

# Lesson 13

## Key Point

Though Jacob was sinful and deceived his brother, God preserved his life and reconciled him with his brother, Esau. Through His Son, God preserves our lives. Jesus overcame sin and death on the cross to win our forgiveness, life, and salvation.

**Draw the parade of presents Jacob sent to Esau. Add family members in back, as described in Genesis 33:1–3. Notice that Jacob led the family group.**

**25–32** Martin Luther described this section of Scripture as among the most obscure passages of the Old Testament. Bible scholars identify Jacob's opponent as God Himself or God's Son, a theophany or appearance of God.

Jacob prayerfully wrestled with God both spiritually and physically. Jacob did not let go, even after God injured his hip. By faith, Jacob clung to God and asked for His blessing. **With what new name did God bless Jacob?** Israel

Jacob means "deceiver," a fitting name for one who stole his brother's birthright and blessing. The new name means "one who wrestles with God and wins." **How did the new name show Jacob's trust in God?** Rather than depending on his own cleverness or deceptions, Jacob trusted God and His promises. He learned to lean on God and His promises.

**Have you ever wrestled with God? What resulted?** Answers vary.

### Part 2: Genesis 33

**1–11** Jacob walked in front of his family to meet Esau. He organized the family in back of him, with Rachel and Joseph farthest from possible danger. **What did Jacob's actions show to Esau?** Jacob bowed seven times, demonstrating respect, humility, submission, and a contrite heart. Jacob called himself his brother's servant (v. 5). He called his brother "lord" (v. 8).

**After a hostile history, how did Esau greet Jacob?** He ran to him, embraced him, hugged him, and kissed him. They both cried. Anger disappeared.

**What do their actions show about their relationship?** They shared forgiveness and acceptance of each other.

**How did God heal this relationship?** Certainly, Jacob worked to reunite with Esau, but God worked to bring reconciliation. He gave Esau willingness to forgive and welcome his brother. Broken relationships result from sin. Sin separates us from God and one another. The Holy Spirit works through God's Word to give us new hearts and minds.

**Why did Jacob say he sent the animals to meet Esau?** To find favor with Esau

**How did Esau respond to the gift?** He protested at first, but agreed when Jacob joyfully persisted in giving these things to his brother.

**What change of heart does Jacob show in verse 11?** Jacob acknowledged that the blessings he tried to steal from Esau years before really came from God. Now reconciled to Esau, he wants to share some of these blessings with Esau.

**12–20** **Why did Jacob want Esau to go on rather than follow him?** The children and nursing flocks needed more time to travel. Jacob encouraged Esau to go ahead and let him follow.

**Esau offered to leave some of the men, probably as protection. Why did Jacob refuse?** Jacob said he had no need. He trusted that God protected him and was with him.

**What is significant about the altar Jacob built and the name he gave it?** Jacob wanted to serve God and live according to his new name, Israel. He called the altar El-Elohe-Israel, which means "God, the God of Israel."

**On your newsprint, write a series of social media posts that tell about the reconciliation between Jacob and Esau and about other chapter 33 details.**

## Debriefing

When time elapses, call everyone back together and ask groups to hang up their work. Ask Part 1 groups to tell about their parade of presents. Ask Part 2 groups to read their social media posts about chapter 33 and the brothers' reconciliation.

Discuss questions students raise from their readings.

# 3 We Live (15 minutes)

## Confession

These questions are not on the Student Page, but the catechism quote is.

**Ask** **Is it easy or hard for you to apologize when you do something wrong?** Let students share.

**Why do you think it is important that we begin worship with Confession and Absolution?** We confess our sinful thoughts, words, and deeds, as well as things we did and things we failed to do. We confess to remind our proud, foolish selves that we were born in sin, we sin every day, and we need a Savior.

The pastor, as a called and ordained servant of God, offers absolution, or forgiveness, to all who confess and believe in Jesus. These are wonderful and blessed assurances of God's love for us in Christ.

Ask students to read the question and answer from Luther's Small Catechism with you (Student Page). Ask the question and ask students to read the answer together.

**Ask** **What sins do we need to confess?** Confession to God, according to the Small Catechism, should be for all sins, even those we don't recognize or recall. If we confess to another individual, we should confess sins we know.

**Say** **There are three types of confession. Let's see if we can name them.** Discuss the following types of confession.

- We can confess privately to a pastor. One benefit is getting to hear the spoken words of absolution personally.

- We can confess to God alone. Tell students that the Lord's Prayer is such a confession. We can also speak to God about any worrisome sins or problems.

- Christians are called to confess their sins to one another. All are guilty of sinning against others. Help students know they can and should go to a person they sin against and confess their sins. A genuine confession is much more than mumbling "Sorry" under your breath.

# 4 Closing (3 minutes)

**Say** **Share something you learned about forgiveness today.** Thank students who share.

**As a closing, repeat the words of 1 John 1:8–9 after me: "If we say we have no sin, / we deceive ourselves, / and the truth is not in us. / If we confess our sins, / He is faithful and just / to forgive us our sins / and to cleanse us from all unrighteousness."**

### Liturgy Link

We have the blessing of Confession and Absolution every week as part of the Divine Service.

### Faith in Action

Encourage students to consider private confession with their pastor. *Lutheran Service Book* includes an order for Individual Confession and Absolution (pp. 292–93).

# Lesson 13
# Esau forgives Jacob

Genesis 31:3; 32:1–33:20

## Journey to reconciliation

**Directions:** Read your assigned verses, discuss questions, and follow directions.

### Part 1: Genesis 32

**Verses 1–2**

- What did the angels' presence tell Jacob?

**Verses 3–8**

- How did Jacob decide to approach Esau?

- What did Esau say in response? What did Jacob think and do about this?

**Verses 9–12**

- Find a main message in each verse of Jacob's prayer to the Lord.

**Verses 13–24**

- What present did Jacob decide to give his brother Esau?

- What strategy did Jacob use to offer the present?

- Draw the parade of presents Jacob sent to Esau. Add family members in back, as described in Genesis 33:1–3. Notice that Jacob led the family group.

**Verses 25–32**

- Martin Luther described this section of Scripture as among the most obscure passages of the Old Testament. Bible scholars identify Jacob's opponent as God Himself or God's Son, a theophany or appearance of God.

  Jacob prayerfully wrestled with God both spiritually and physically. Jacob did not let go, even after God injured his hip. By faith, Jacob clung to God and asked for His blessing. With what new name did God bless Jacob?

- Jacob means "deceiver," a fitting name for one who stole his brother's birthright and blessing. The new name means "one who wrestles with God and wins." How did the new name show Jacob's trust in God?

- Have you ever wrestled with God? What resulted?

### Part 2: Genesis 33

**Verses 1–11**

- Jacob walked in front of his family to meet Esau. He organized the family in back of him, with Rachel and Joseph farthest from possible danger. What did Jacob's actions show to Esau?

- After a hostile history, how did Esau greet Jacob?

- What do their actions show about their relationship?

- How did God heal this relationship?

- Why did Jacob say he sent the animals to meet Esau?

- How did Esau respond to the gift?

- What change of heart does Jacob show in verse 11?

**Verses 12–20**

- Why did Jacob want Esau to go on rather than follow him?

- Esau offered to leave some of the men, probably as protection. Why did Jacob refuse?

- What is significant about the altar Jacob built and the name he gave it?

- Write a series of social media posts that tell about the reconciliation between Jacob and Esau and about other chapter 33 details.

## Luther's Small Catechism

### What is confession?

Confession has two parts.

First, that we confess our sins, and

second, that we receive absolution, that is, forgiveness, from the pastor as from God Himself, not doubting, but firmly believing that by it our sins are forgiven before God in heaven.